Praise for

Discipled Warriors Handbook

How many times have you asked yourself, "What is God's purpose and plan for me?". Every man I deeply know has asked this, or a similar question, several times throughout his adult life; I certainly have. In the *Discipled Warriors Handbook*, Dr. Ray Dillman has created 26 "bite-sized" lessons that aid in the knowledge, understanding, and application of God's word for men to live a God-centered and mission-driven life. These lesson topics offer profound insights that can reshape your life and the purpose God has for you.

Over the past 30 years, I've had the opportunity to train thousands of men in a variety of disciplines related to our national defense, contributing to a continued projection of strength and sovereignty. As Jesus-followers, our legacy is centered on The Great Commission, found in Matthew 28:19-20, which God has given to each of us. Ray's "Discipled Warriors" teachings have significantly helped me, and many others, in equipping and educating for this personal Commission. More than reading material, this is an enduring spiritual journey of God's specific plan He has for you.

—**Mark McGuckin**, US Navy (Ret)

***

Who is God? How can I trust what the Bible teaches? How can I be the man God wants me to be? The *Discipled Warriors Handbook* is a transformational guide that leads us men in understanding who God is and how we can be the men God created us to be. This expertly crafted, biblically based program helps us understand our role as defined by Scripture and teaches us how to lead our lives to be the men that God intended for our families, our communities, and ourselves. This *Handbook* is a must-have for any man or group of men seeking strong, Christ-centered guidance to live meaningful lives in an increasingly turbulent world. I've personally witnessed the Discipled Warrior program bring powerful and positive change to men's lives, as well as my own, and it will do the same for you. Use this invaluable guide to become the man God intends you to be.

—**Evan Ellis**, Manager Network Services – *AT&T*

***

There are times when you know that God is working through someone. Discipled Warriors is a ministry that God has called Ray Dillman to lead. I have seen the difference it has made in other men as well as myself. The *Discipled Warriors Handbook* captures the ministry by providing lessons that encourage men to connect with one another for friendship, accountability, encouragement, and challenge. I have personally seen this happen for the men who have gone through Discipled Warriors training. I would encourage any man to go through the study, especially if you don't want to. I challenge you to invest the time to work through the lessons offered in the *Discipled Warriors Handbook*, with a group of men or by yourself, and see what God can do for you, your marriage, and your family.

—**Bruce Christian**, Senior Pastor, *Woodland Hills Baptist Church*

***

In a world where men are often left to, or worse, believe that they must figure things out on their own, Dr. Ray Dillman's *Discipled Warriors Handbook* seeks to bring guidance and camaraderie in every facet of life. Having known and worked with Ray, I have personally seen his commitment to Jesus Christ, his family, and his passion for equipping men. He understands that men need not only a heart for God but also the tools to pursue Him.

Grounded in the inspiration and authority of Scripture, Dr. Dillman provides an insightful understanding of God and His design for men. Comprehensive in nature, *Discipled Warriors Handbook* also addresses many critical areas that men need to address with courageous vulnerability, doing so in a challenging yet highly relatable way. This kind of handbook is needed and would be highly effective for those who are serious about becoming the husbands, fathers, and servant leaders that God is calling them to be.

—**Dr. Justin Key**, Chair, School of Ministry, *Mid-America Christian University*

Discipled Warriors Handbook

Ray Dillman, PhD
Major (US Army, Ret)

Published by KHARIS PUBLISHING, an imprint of
KHARIS MEDIA LLC.

ISBN-13: 978-1-63746-669-8

ISBN-10: 1-63746-669-2

Library of Congress Control Number: 2026935185

All KHARIS PUBLISHING products are available at special quantity discounts for bulk purchases for sales promotions, premiums, fund-raising, and educational needs. For details, contact:

Kharis Media LLC
Tel: +1 (331) 312-2376
support@kharispublishing.com
www.kharispublishing.com

Dedication

"To the fearless disciples of Jesus."

Contents

Table of Figures

Introduction

Discipled Warriors Ministry

The Discipled Warriors Ministry supports the Church by providing men with a clear answer to the question: "Why am I here?" The ministry uses a variety of platforms to teach and train men to become who God created them to be—His Discipled Warriors.

This handbook is an extension of the ministry's in-person platforms, the two-day intensive program, and the one-day conference. For men unable to attend a Discipled Warriors in-person platform, the ministry offers the handbook as a form of self-study. Discipled Warriors Podcasts are an additional resource for program content.

How to Use the Handbook

If you are unfamiliar with Discipled Warriors material and are using the handbook as a self-study, complete the lessons sequentially. The Discipled Warriors' educational programming builds upon fundamental truths to create understanding of the complexities of spiritual warfare. Thus, a later lesson's content may not make sense if you did not understand the content from a previous lesson. Cover the handbook's lessons in sequence. Allocate about one hour for each lesson. Many lessons contain substantial theological information that could require significant time for you to think through and comprehend. Look up each lesson's provided Scripture to biblically reinforce the truths presented. Use the blank page at the end of each lesson to capture your written responses to Lesson Applications and whatever other insights you gain from the lesson. Later lessons will ask you to refer back to previous responses.

For questions, concerns, or comments about this book's material, please email ray@discipledwarriors.org. I will respond as soon as possible.

Ray Dillman, Ph.D.

Major, US Army (Retired)

Lesson 1

How Do We Know God Exists?

The first lesson in the Discipled Warriors educational program is: How Do We Know God Exists? We start here because it is a question all people must answer at some point. God–or the existence of some form of a higher power–is a commonly understood concept. It is something all people have considered. We'll start the lesson with a summary of what common understanding means.

Common Understanding

When we are born into this world, we are endowed with five senses associated with the organs that are generally present in all people. We have eyes to see, ears to hear, a nose to smell, a tongue to taste, and skin to feel. Our five senses are used to experience and collect information about the world we inhabit; however, our senses perceive the world slightly differently.

For example, while most people can distinguish between short and long objects, agreeing on a specific length is very difficult. Another example of the difficulties of common understanding is weight determination. Having two people agree upon the specific weight of an unknown object is a very difficult proposition. Yet another example is taste. While most people can tell if something is salty or sweet, hardly anyone will agree on a specific level of saltiness or sweetness.

The point is that while our five senses are generally the same among all people, our senses display slight differences between individuals. Since we all have slightly different abilities within our five natural senses, having us experience the same reality associated with seeing, hearing, smelling, tasting, and touching is mathematically impossible because we don't have a natural way to quantify those slight differences with agreed-upon standards.

Let's reuse the salty example to explain quantification. Suppose we all taste something very salty. What does "very salty" mean? "Very" is not a measurement everyone commonly understands because it is not quantifiable. It means different amounts to different people.

Attaining a common understanding demands measurement tools that provide standardized information. Tools that all users agree on are considered reliable and valid. A reliable tool produces the same results no matter how it is used. A valid tool accurately measures what it is supposed to measure.

An example of a reliable and valid measurement tool is a ruler. A ruler is reliable because it measures the length or width of an object using inches or centimeters as the measurement standard. A ruler is valid because the labeled inches or centimeters can be easily verified. Thus, rulers are reliable and valid measurement instruments that provide a common understanding among users of rulers.

Another reliable and valid measurement instrument is a weight scale. The scale is reliable because it measures the weight of an object in pounds or kilograms. The scale is valid because pounds or kilograms are units that can easily be verified.

Experiences Outside of Natural Senses

Supernatural is the term we use for what we know exists outside our natural senses. Unlike the ruler or the scale, we cannot rely upon our senses to provide a common understanding of the supernatural, such as God. Yet, every recorded civilization has some form of recognizing deity, despite not being able to see, hear, smell, taste, or touch the supernatural presence.

Likely, you have personally experienced God, experienced something that can only be explained by the existence of God, or know of someone who claims to have experienced God. Which of the five senses is used to provide a common understanding of God for all people? The answer is that none of our five senses can detect and measure God's existence in a way that provides a common understanding.

It is apparent that all humans recognize something outside of the natural world around us. Children who believe in Santa Claus, the Easter Bunny, and the Tooth Fairy display a belief in knowing there is something more than we can naturally sense. We see evidence of adults exhibiting a belief in the existence of something beyond our natural senses in the multitude of movies, TV shows, and books that feature people or objects with unique, unnatural powers. Examples of adults trying to explain what is not natural include the ideas of time travel, fantasy worlds, and magical powers.

Another observation about the existence of the supernatural from every recorded civilization is the recognition of basic moral truths. All societies exhibit some form of civil structure that allows the group to function over long periods of time. One of the fundamental moral truths that underpins a healthy, functioning society is the idea that families—particularly nuclear families—are essential to a healthy society. On the other hand, actions that are detrimental to a healthy society include lying, stealing, rape, and murder.

Our natural senses cannot reliably or validly measure the moral truths exhibited in every society throughout history. Another way to think about those truths is that they are supernatural—outside our natural senses. How complex would a tool need to be to explain why all societies have demonstrated these core moral beliefs? The tool would have to be more complex than a ruler or weight scale because there are many more factors to measure than one observation.

Explaining the Unmeasurable

Documents are the tools for explaining the supernatural and complex basic moral truths. The Discipled Warriors Ministry solely uses the Bible to explain the supernatural and basic moral truths we all know exist. The ministry has examined similar documents and considers them fraudulent and a waste of time.

The Bible explains the supernatural and fundamental moral truths with two verses. In Ecclesiastes 3:11, Solomon wrote that God "...has put eternity into man's heart." In other words, everyone who has ever existed knows there is something more to this world than what our five senses can detect. In Romans 1:18-20, Paul wrote, "What can be known about God is plain to them, because God has shown it to them. For his invisible attributes, namely, his eternal power and divine nature, have been clearly perceived, ever since the creation of the world, in the things that have been made. So they are without excuse" [for] "ungodliness and unrighteousness of men, who by their unrighteousness suppress the truth." The Bible states that everyone recognizes the fundamental moral truths common to all people and civilizations.

The Bible opens with this verse: "In the beginning, God created the heavens and the earth" (Genesis 1:1). So, God created everything our five senses can detect. Second Timothy 3:16's opening phrase states, "God breathes out all Scripture..." Combining these two verses explains the Bible as a document written by the very Creator of this world.

In other words, our Creator wrote a document we call the Bible that explains supernatural phenomena and basic moral truths that we cannot measure using our five natural senses. Several passages bolster this explanation by referring to the Bible as the Word of God, including Psalm 119, Proverbs 30:5, Isaiah 40:8 and 55:11, Jeremiah 23:29, John 17:17, Romans 10:17, Ephesians 6:17, and Hebrews 4:12. A basic tenet of the Christian faith is that God wrote the Bible.

The next question is: Can we trust the Bible to provide a common understanding upon which we can all agree? In other words, is the Bible reliable? Can we trust the Bible to provide consistent measurements? And, is the Bible valid? Does it use measurements upon which we all agree?

Since the beginning of the early church following the death, resurrection, and ascension of our Lord Jesus Christ, tens of thousands of smart and talented people have spent their entire professional careers in a field we call *apologetics*. Apologetics is the logical defense of the Christian faith and—by extension—the reliability and validity of the Bible. The field of apologetics contains numerous solid, logical, apologetic arguments for God, Jesus, the Holy Spirit, and the Bible.

For example, the *Discipled Warriors Handbook* could be considered an apologetic argument, however, no matter how good an argument is, each person has to make a personal choice to believe in the veracity or truthfulness of the Bible. Ultimately, believing the Bible is the one document God wrote to explain the supernatural and fundamental moral truths we all know exist requires a leap of faith.

The Bible Explains God's Existence

This lesson's opening question was, how do we know God exists? Historically, all societies have demonstrated a belief in the existence of the supernatural. The Bible—the document written by God specifically for us to understand the supernatural and basic moral truths—also explains God's existence. For example, John 4:24 states "God is spirit." In other words, God is not part of this physical world.

God is supernatural, which we know exists but cannot be routinely detected by our five natural senses. When we experience Him with one of our senses, we cannot explain the experience in a way that provides common understanding to others.

The Bible provides us with an intellectual knowledge of God's existence in a way that can be commonly understood. We still have to choose to believe what the Bible says, but once we do, we can begin to acquire an experiential understanding of Him. Knowing the Bible and believing what it says allows us to see God's character, power, and will at work in our lives.

Combining our intellectual and experiential understanding of God allows us to have what we and God ultimately want: A personal, intimate, and peaceful relationship highlighted by unconditional love. Accepting God's unconditional love is the only way anyone will have supernatural peace, which we all long for. In John 16:33, Jesus told His disciples, "I have said these things to you, that in me you may have peace." Having God's peace begins with believing what the Bible says about His existence.

If you are having trouble believing the Bible as the single source of truth in this world, search out and review some trustworthy apologetic arguments. Ultimately, you will have to take a leap of faith in the document's truthfulness. If you have difficulty trusting the Bible, do what the man struggling with his faith did when he met Jesus in Mark

9:24: Ask God to help you with your unbelief. The Bible tells us God exists and provides a common understanding of His existence.

Lesson Application - Write down how you know God exists. What experiences or revelations have you had that led you to believe in the existence of God?

Lesson 2

Why I Trust the Bible

Context

The previous lesson's application asked you to write down your personal experience(s) with knowing the existence of God. Having a personal experience should lead you to want to know God more. The Bible is the source document for an improved understanding of God.

Intellectually knowing the Bible speaks about God, however, is different than believing the Bible speaks about God. We must understand and explain why we believe in the Bible's validity. This lesson explains why I believe the Bible is true. You might find my reasoning aligns with why you believe the Bible is true. Search for apologetic arguments on the Bible's validity if you want to see other people's reasoning. There are multitudes of arguments to be found.

Bible Facts

Let's start with facts with which no Bible scholar nor informed atheist would disagree. An accurate, inarguable description of the Bible is that it is a collection of sixty-six books written by forty men over 1,500 years in three different languages on three continents. We'll take each of those descriptions one at a time.

First, while people often refer to the Bible as a book, a more accurate description is that it is a canon, an anthology, or a collection of different books. Further, each of those sixty-six books is literary in nature, meaning they are written documents. Stylistically, the books are different. In literary analysis, we call these stylistic differences genres.

The genres of the books include historical pieces, narrative stories, poetry, parables, prophecy, sermons, wisdom literature, gospels, letters, epistles, and apocalyptic literature. Readers of biblical books not only have to understand that there are different genres, but also different styles of writing. Sometimes, the writing style is literal such as "You shall not murder" in Exodus 20:13. Sometimes the writing style is figurative where the idea presented has a different meaning than the words used. Figurative language includes metaphor, simile, personification, or hyperbole. A biblical example of a metaphor is "God shelters us with His wings" in Psalm 91:4.

The forty men who penned the biblical books represent various cultures, societies, historical eras, and professional backgrounds. The professional backgrounds of the men include shepherds, kings, priests, prophets, fishermen, tax collectors, and doctors.

They spoke different languages and lived in different time frames in different parts of the world. The three languages in which the books were written were Hebrew, Aramaic, and Greek. Because the books were written over a 1,500-year timeframe, most of the men who penned the books never met the other men who contributed to the collection. Not only were the men separated by time, but they were also separated by space, and the books were written on three different continents: Africa, Asia, and Europe.

All of the facts I just laid out are indisputable about the Bible. It is the most scrutinized document in human history, particularly when it comes to its origin and authenticity. Even though the biblical canon has been thoroughly reviewed, there has never been an accepted argument that disproves the Bible's origin or authenticity.

Now let's look at some nuances about the Bible. First, if you have ever studied a different language, you know that words and concepts do not always seamlessly translate from one language to another. Each language has nuances associated with it that reflect its unique culture and traditions, yet the forty men who penned the Bible in three different languages on three different continents across 1,500 years provide a cohesive message.

Cohesive does not mean identical. A great example of a cohesive message is the four Gospels. Matthew, Mark, Luke, and John share a cohesive message about the birth, teachings, miracles, death, and resurrection of Jesus. Additionally, all four books state that Jesus fulfilled many Old Testament prophecies about the Jewish Messiah.

Let's expand from the four Gospels to the entire biblical collection. The cohesive message of the Bible's sixty-six books is the creation, fall, and redemption of mankind. All of the books share the common message that salvation is available to all who repent of their sins and commit to following God with all their heart, soul, mind, and strength. To add to the infinitely miraculous common storyline, theme, and message, the sixty-six books contain no historical errors or contradictions.

My Experience

Now that I have laid out the facts of the Bible, I need to discuss my professional background to explain how my experience informs my belief in the Bible as the complete truth. My first professional career was in the Army. I enlisted as a private, and after 23 years of military service, I retired as a major. Most of my service was spent in infantry and special operations units, and I was considered an expert in planning for and executing tactical missions such as raids and ambushes. The military units I was in used mission statements to accomplish our tasks.

The mission statement provides a task and purpose. The task is what the unit will accomplish, and the purpose is why the unit needs to accomplish the task. The mission statement provides an overarching goal for every unit member to understand how to support the unit. In my time, mission statements were written down, discussed in open forums, and rehearsed to ensure a common understanding among all unit members. Every unit member knew the mission statement verbatim and how he/she supported accomplishing the unit's mission.

My second career was in higher education. A large portion of that 13-year career was spent as an English professor. As a professor, I taught numerous literature courses. This helps explain my understanding of the Bible as a literary document. However, my particular expertise as an English professor is composition, which is teaching college students how to write narrative essays, research papers, and arguments. I have taught around fifty different writing courses, which have included approximately 750 students. When it comes to teaching composition, I am considered an expert. Based on my experience, a common understanding of a specific topic is highly unusual.

For example, if I were to give a class of twenty students the same writing prompt, such as "Provide an argument for why the Bible is important to a Christian education," I can assure you I would get twenty different arguments. Twenty different students, all in the same class, writing a paper on the same topic that comes from a single source, will all produce different arguments.

I have observed two opposite methods of interpreting messages in my professional background and expertise. In the military, all members commonly share the same message, known as the mission statement. The members would all repeat the mission statement's message, word for word. In my educational experience, all members interpret the same message differently, which is understandable given their diverse backgrounds, interests, and abilities. These differences are inherent to God's creation—no two creations are identical.

So, my professional experience tells me that a message only maintains integrity from person to person when there is a collective will to repeat the message. When an individual is allowed to interpret the message, the message will change.

An example many of us are familiar with of how a message changes from person to person is the telephone game. The game begins with a group of people sitting in a circle. One person whispers something to the next person. That person then attempts to repeat what they heard (or thought they heard) to the next person. This continues from one person to the next until the end, when the last person tells the group what they heard.

I played the game a few times in elementary school, and the ending message was never the same as the starting message. I'm told the game is a good ice-breaker for showing how a collection of adults will all interpret a given message differently.

Combining Biblical Facts with Personal Expertise

I have covered the inarguable facts of the Bible and my professional expertise. Once I mixed the Bible's facts with my professional expertise, I became convinced the Bible could only have been produced supernaturally. My experience as a professor tells me that different people produce vastly different messages. My experience in the military tells me that the only way the same message gets repeated is when there is a collective will behind it. And when there is a collective will, the message is exactly the same among all members.

As a literary document, the Bible features forty distinct writing personalities or voices, yet maintains a cohesive message. In my professional opinion, there is no way a group of forty men could have produced a document that not only shows their individual personalities, cultures, and languages but also produces the same messages in each of the sixty-six books. I can only attribute my realization of the document's uniqueness to the collective will that expresses a cohesive message in a way that allows the individual personalities of the men who penned it to be conveyed.

Second Timothy 3:16 and 2 Peter 1:19-21 tell us God inspired the entire document we call the Bible; thus, God's Holy Spirit provided the collective will for each of the men who penned their respective books. His collective will is why the Bible has a common theme and message across the sixty-six books contained in the collection.

If the Bible is truly the inspired Word of God, then His Holy Spirit, which provided the collective will for a common message spanning 1,500 years across three languages, three continents, and forty men, can provide each of us the same certainty of authenticity. Having certainty in the veracity of the Bible is necessary for a believer's spiritual growth. For me, the Bible's certainty as the only source of truth in this world provides the solid ground I need to make sense of a world that often makes no sense.

Assurance that the Bible is true is also why I can confidently provide this lesson. I know God's Holy Spirit inspired the Bible. I am able to stand on truth when I share God's message with others. If you have not reached the same conclusion that I have reached—that the Bible is God's message to all humanity and can be wholly trusted as the one and only source of truth in this world—then I have a couple of questions for you:

Where does truth come from?

What is your solid ground?

If you don't have something you can rely on to tell you the truth, no matter what, you don't have solid ground. You will wander through this life lost, like flotsam on ocean currents. If you are lost, pray about your hesitancy. Ask God to allow you to be confident in the Bible's veracity. Also, don't neglect to use your experience and the brain God has given you to think about whether the Bible's message is true. Be an explorer of the Bible and ask hard questions. God is big enough to handle whatever questions you have.

Lesson Application - Write down your thoughts on the veracity of the Bible. Why do you believe it's true? If you don't believe it's 100 percent true, write down your reasons. Then, ask God to show you the truth about those reasons in quiet prayer. Again, if God is truly God, He knows whether you trust the Bible or not, so be honest with Him.

Lesson 3

The Trinity

Context

The previous lesson covered one argument for trusting the Bible. The argument summarizes that readers can distinguish the unique personalities of the forty men in the books they penned, yet their sixty-six books maintain a cohesive message of mankind's creation, fall, and redemption. Those 40 authors could only have accomplished that cohesive message by a single, all-powerful will that allowed the men to express their unique personalities. This lesson begins an exploration of the single, all-powerful will that authored the Bible.

Proverbs 1:7 states, "The fear of the Lord is the beginning of knowledge; fools despise wisdom and instruction." In order to be fearful of the Lord, we must know how He is. The Bible tells us the LORD God has many identities that inform us of who He is. One of the ways the Bible discusses God is by displaying His three distinct persons: the Father, the Son, and the Holy Spirit.

New Testament Trinity

Numerous New Testament (NT) passages display what biblical experts refer to as the Holy Trinity. One passage containing the Trinity is 2 Corinthians 13:14, "The grace of the Lord Jesus Christ and the love of

God and the fellowship of the Holy Spirit be with you all." The verse, which was written by the Apostle Paul, contains the three persons we know as God.

Peter, another apostle, also grouped the Trinity in one of his letters. First Peter 1:2 states, "According to the foreknowledge of God the Father, in the sanctification of the Spirit, for obedience to Jesus Christ and for sprinkling with his blood: May grace and peace be multiplied to you."

In John 14:26, the Apostle John quotes Jesus as saying, "But the Helper, the Holy Spirit, whom the Father will send in my name, he will teach you all things and bring to your remembrance all that I have said to you."

One of the clearest NT examples of the distinct but equal personalities of the Trinity is found in Matthew 28:19, which states, "Go therefore and make disciples of all nations, baptizing them in the name of the Father and of the Son and of the Holy Spirit." This verse is part of the Great Commission that Jesus gave His disciples at the end of His ministry.

Matthew, another apostle, also shows the Trinity at the beginning of Jesus's ministry, stating, "And when Jesus was baptized, immediately he went up from the water, and behold, the heavens were opened to him, and he saw the Spirit of God descending like a dove and coming to rest on him; and behold, a voice from heaven said, 'This is my beloved Son, with whom I am well pleased.'" In the baptism passage, Jesus has the Holy Spirit descending on Him while His Heavenly Father declares Jesus as His beloved Son.

It is not a coincidence that Matthew bookends Jesus's ministry with a display of the Trinity. The audience for his gospel was his fellow Jews–the very people who would be most familiar with the Scriptures before the time of Jesus, which is what we currently call the Old Testament (OT).

Old Testament Trinity

While the NT explicitly displays the Trinity, OT passages are more implicit in their display of the Triune God. Isaiah 42:1-9 is one OT passage where the three persons are grouped together.

> [1] Behold my servant, whom I uphold, / my chosen, in whom my soul delights; I have put my Spirit upon him; he will bring forth justice to the nations. [2] He will not cry aloud or lift up his voice, or make it heard in the street; [3] a bruised reed he will not break, and a faintly burning wick he will not quench; he will faithfully bring forth justice. [4] He will not grow faint or be discouraged till he has established justice in the earth; and the coastlands wait for his law. [5] Thus says God, the Lord, who created the heavens and stretched them out, who spread out the earth and what comes from it, who gives breath to the people on it and spirit to those who walk in it: [6] "I am the Lord; I have called you in righteousness; I will take you by the hand and keep you; will give you as a covenant for the people, a light for the nations, [7] to open the eyes that are blind, to bring out the prisoners from the dungeon, from the prison those who sit in darkness. [8] I am the Lord; that is my name; my glory I give to no other, nor my praise to carved idols. [9] Behold, the former things have come to pass, and new things I now declare; before they spring forth I tell you of them.

In verses one to four, this passage discusses how God's chosen servant in whom He delights will have God's Spirit. Verse 5 states that the God who created the heavens and earth is the One who will place His Spirit on the servant, and verse 8 states that He will not share His glory. Reasoning tells us that the servant in whom the creator delights and will have God's Spirit is Jesus. I say reasoning because verse 8 tells us God does not share His glory, thus, the servant and the Spirit must also be God. Using reason and biblical substantiation, we can see that the passage of Isaiah 42:1-9 groups the three persons of the Trinity—just not as explicitly as the previously covered NT passages.

The OT clearly indicates that God is more than one person. In the first book of the Bible, Genesis 1:26, we read, "Then God said, 'Let us make man in our image, after our likeness.'" Later, in Genesis 3:22, we read, "Then the LORD God said, 'Behold, the man has become like one of us in knowing good and evil.'" One more Genesis passage shows God using the pronoun "us" in describing Himself. In Genesis 11:7, we read, "Come, let us go down and there confuse their language, so that they may not understand one another's speech."

The use of the pronoun "us" in three passages of the Bible's opening book strongly indicates that God views Himself as more than one entity. Proverbs 30:4 is another OT passage that shows God as more than one person. The verse states, "What is his name, and what is his son's name?" The line displays God in two persons—the Father and the Son—who have the same power and authority. Let's examine some OT passages where the Father, Spirit, and Son are individually stated.

The Father in the Old Testament

The OT passages on God as the Father begin with Deuteronomy 32:6, which states, "Do you thus repay the Lord, / you foolish and senseless people? / Is not he your father, who created you, / who made you and established you?" Other OT passages showing God as the Father include Psalm 103:13, Proverbs 3:12, Isaiah 63:16, Isaiah 64:8, Jeremiah 3:19, Jeremiah 31:9, and Malachi 1:6. The last OT passage that shows God as the Father is Malachi 2:10, which states, "Have we not all one Father? Has not one God created us? Why then are we faithless to one another, profaning the covenant of our fathers?"

The Spirit in the Old Testament

God, as the Holy Spirit, is also displayed in the OT. Genesis 1:2, Job 26:13, and Psalm 104:30 show the Spirit was instrumental in Creation.

Genesis 6:3 tells us God's Spirit is necessary for a person's continued existence in this world.

The OT often shows God's Spirit was upon certain judges, warriors, and prophets in a way that gave them extraordinary power. Examples include Numbers 27:18, Judges 3:10, 6:34, 13:25, 14:6, and 1 Samuel 10:9-10. The OT often speaks of the Spirit being poured out on people as a blessing. This can be seen in Proverbs 1:23, Isaiah 32:15 and 44:3, Joel 2:28, and Zechariah 12:10.

In Ezekiel 36:27, we see that God's Spirit will be placed inside His people. The verse states, "And I will put my Spirit within you, and cause you to walk in my statutes and be careful to obey my rules." First Samuel 16:14 shows us that disobedience can also remove God's Spirit from a person—in this case, King Saul: "Now the Spirit of the LORD departed from Saul."

Jesus in the Old Testament

To begin a discussion on Jesus in the OT, we need to understand why the Bible sometimes uses all capital letters to write the word LORD. The LORD talked face-to-face with Moses in the burning bush story in Exodus 3. When Moses asked for the LORD's name, the LORD said, "I AM WHO I AM" in Exodus 3:14. The Hebrew name for I AM is pronounced Yahweh. The Latinized pronunciation is Jehovah. Both names represent the covenant name of God.

In Genesis 18:1-33, the LORD appeared in human form and talked to Abraham. In Exodus 33:17-23, the same capitalized LORD—Yahweh or Jehovah—told Moses that man could not see Him and live. This begs the question of how Yahweh could appear in front of and talk to Abraham, but could not appear before Moses without Moses dying?

The only explanation for the same Yahweh appearing in human form to Abraham but not appearing before Moses is that God must be expressed in at least two persons. The Yahweh who talked to Abraham in Genesis 18 had to be a different representation of God than the one who talked to Moses in Exodus 33. Because we benefit from having the NT, we know from John 10:30 that Jesus stated He and the Father are one. Thus, the LORD who spoke to, but could not appear before, Moses in Exodus 33 was the Father, while the LORD who talked to and appeared before Abraham in Genesis 18 was Jesus. Many Bible scholars believe that passages discussing the angel of the LORD are Christophanies—appearances of the pre-incarnate Jesus in human form.[1,2]

OT passages where the appearance of the angel of the LORD can be seen include Genesis 16:7-14, 18:1-33, and 22:11-18, Exodus 3:2, Judges 2:1-4, 5:23, 6:11-24, and 13:3-22, 2 Samuel 24:16, 2 Kings 19:35, Zechariah 1:12, 3:1, and 12:8.

Pre-incarnate Jesus is represented in other OT passages that don't use the phrase "the angel of the LORD." For example, in Joshua 5:13-15, Joshua worships the "commander of the army of the LORD" and is not rebuked for his worship. Another example is in Daniel 3:25, when Nebuchadnezzar saw a fourth person in the fire with Shadrach, Meshach, and Abednego, who had "the appearance…like a son of the gods."

---

[1] Stewart, Don. "Who Is the Angel of the Lord in the Old Testament?" Blue Letter Bible.https://www.blueletterbible.org/faq/don_stewart/don_stewart_26.cfm

[2] "Who is the Angel of the LORD? 8 solid proofs he is Jesus." Cornerstone Verses. April 27, 2024. https://cornerstoneverses.com/the-angel-of-the-lord/

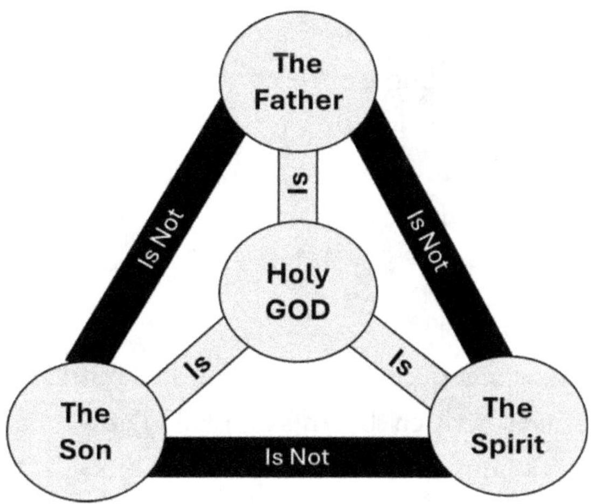

Figure 1 - The Holy Trinity

Jesus fulfills OT Scripture

We have looked at numerous OT passages that express God in singular forms of the Father, Spirit, and pre-incarnate Jesus. When Jesus becomes incarnate in the NT, He does not change, override, or discount the books of the OT—quite the opposite. The 27 books of the NT fulfill and clarify the 39 books we currently refer to as the OT. Jewish society in the time of Jesus referred to the OT as the Law and the Prophets.

Matthew 5:17 tells us that while giving His Sermon on the Mount, Jesus stated, "Do not think that I have come to abolish the Law or the Prophets; I have not come to abolish them but to fulfill them." In Jesus's own words, He fulfills what is written in the OT. Another NT passage confirming Jesus as the fulfillment of OT Scripture is Luke 24:44. In this passage, Jesus appeared to His disciples after His resurrection and told them, "These are my words that I spoke to you while I was still with you, that everything written about me in the Law of Moses and the Prophets and the Psalms must be fulfilled."

John 5 is another NT passage that shows Jesus as clarifying and fulfilling what is stated in the OT. The chapter opens with Jesus healing a paralytic man in Jerusalem on the Sabbath. Religious Jews then persecuted Jesus for healing on the Sabbath and for stating God was His Father in verse 17. Jesus attempts to educate His persecutors in verse 39 by stating, "You search the Scriptures because you think that in them you have eternal life; and it is they that bear witness about me." He adds in verse 46, "For if you believed Moses, you would believe me; for he wrote of me."

While the Gospels quote Jesus stating He fulfilled OT Scripture, other NT passages written by the Apostle Paul attest to the same fulfillment. In Philippians 3:5, Paul called himself "a Hebrew of Hebrews" and "a Pharisee," meaning he would have been intimately familiar with Scripture. Paul concluded that faith in Jesus as the Messiah promised in Scripture allowed all people to be included as heirs of the Abrahamic Covenant, which was originally expressed in Genesis 17:1-8. See Romans 4 and Galatians 3 for two other passages of Scripture that explicitly state how Christ fulfilled the Abrahamic Covenant.

Summary

To reiterate, the lesson aimed to understand who authored the collection of the sixty-six books we call the Bible, but it does not attempt to explain the Holy Trinity in a way that makes sense. Understanding how three separate individuals can simultaneously form one entity is beyond human comprehension. According to 1 Kings 3:12, God gave Solomon more wisdom and discernment than anyone who ever existed.

In Ecclesiastes 8:17, Solomon wrote, "I also saw all that God has done. Nobody can understand what God does here on earth. No matter how hard people try to understand it, they cannot. Even if wise people say they understand, they cannot; no one can really understand it." Sometimes, we must accept the fact that we cannot fully comprehend God. What we *can* understand is that the Old and New

Testaments show God in three equal but distinct persons: the Father, the Son, and the Spirit.

Lesson Application - Describe your personal understanding of each person within the Trinity. Write down what you remember about any moments you have had with any of the three.

If you have not had a personal experience with one or more of the persons of the Trinity, write down a prayer request you can make about your desire to meet. Later lessons teach how to maximize your prayer time with God, and will ask you to reference what you wrote down in this lesson.

Lesson 4

The Father

Context

The previous lesson presented the Bible's authorship, focusing on the Triune God as discussed in the Old and New Testament scripture passages. This lesson begins a three-part series on the Trinity's three individual identities. The first identity we'll cover is the Father.

Understanding who authored the Bible is essential to trusting what the Bible states. I trust the Bible because only a supernatural power could have maintained a consistent message that spans multiple books, penned by a wide variety of men whose unique personalities are evident in the words they wrote. For example, the epistles of Peter, Paul, James, and John convey similar messages, even though their distinct personalities are evident in the words they penned to express these unified themes. Another example can be found in the books of Isaiah, Jeremiah, and Ezekiel. All three books contain prophecies related to the Babylonian captivity while allowing the unique personalities of the three prophets to be maintained.

Father

God, as the capital "F" Father, is found throughout the Bible, including Deuteronomy 32:6, Psalm 103:13, Proverbs 3:12, Isaiah 63:16, Malachi 2:10, Matthew 28:19, 1 Peter 1:2, and Revelation 3:5.

God the Father is also revealed and identified by at least thirty-four other names in Scripture. This lesson provides the names in an accepted version of the original Hebrew, along with the English translation found in the Bible. Finally, each example includes a passage of Scripture that contains the name. The primary source used for Hebrew translations was the Blue Letter Bible (blueletterbible.org).

1. *Yahweh* is the Hebrew name for "I AM WHO I AM" or "the LORD" in all capital letters. When we see the word LORD in all caps, we need to recognize this is our English translation's way of identifying the covenant name of God, first spoken to Moses in Exodus 3:14, which states, "God said to Moses, 'I AM WHO I AM.' And he said, 'Say this to the people of Israel: 'I AM has sent me to you.''' Jews write the covenant name using the capital letters YHWH. The pronunciation of Yahweh is produced by adding vowels to the capital letters.

   Yehovah is another variant of the acronym YHWH, and another acceptable way to say God's covenant name. The Latinized form of Yahweh or Yehovah is to change the "Y" to a "J" and pronounce the name *Jehovah*. All three names, Yahweh, Yehovah, and Jehovah, mean "The LORD" in all capital letters.

2. *Adonai* is the Hebrew name for "Lord," where only the "L" is capitalized. Adonai can also be interpreted as "Master." An example verse is Psalm 8:1, which has both the LORD in all caps and the Lord where only the "L" is capitalized. Here is the verse, "O LORD [in all caps], our Lord [only the L is capitalized], how majestic is your name in all the earth! You have set your glory above the heavens."

"El" Names

In Hebrew, the word "el" means god, lowercase "g." Capitalizing the "e" is another way to indicate the God capital "g." The Bible has four names for Father God using the prefix "El."

3. *Elohim* (el-o-heem') is the Hebrew name for "God" or "gods." An example verse is Genesis 1:1, which states, "In the beginning, God [Elohim] created the heavens and the earth."

4. *El Olam* (o-lawm'), in English, is "The everlasting God" or "the eternal God." An example verse is Genesis 21:33, which states, "Abraham planted a tamarisk tree in Beersheba and called there on the name of the LORD, the Everlasting God [Olam]."

5. *El Roi* (ro-ee') is interpreted as "The God who sees." The example verse is Genesis 16:13, which states, "So she called the name of the LORD who spoke to her, 'You are a God of seeing,' for she said, 'Truly here I have seen him who looks after me.'"

6. *El Shaddai* (shad-dah'-ee) is "God Almighty" or "God the All-Powerful." An example verse is found in Genesis 17:1. "When Abram was ninety-nine years old the LORD appeared to Abram and said to him, 'I am God Almighty; walk before me, and be blameless.'"

Jehovah Names

The next 28 names begin with Jehovah, the Latinized form of the all-capitalized "LORD." As a reminder, Yahweh or Yehovah are the other acceptable names we could use for the all-capitalized "LORD" since they also represent the covenant name of God.

Jehovah is likely the more familiar name used for the Great "I AM" due to its usage in the King James Version of the Bible. The name following Jehovah is a version of the original Hebrew.

7. *Jehovah Chereb* (kheh'-reb) means "The LORD the sword." An example verse is Deuteronomy 33:29, which states, "Happy are you, O Israel! Who is like you, a people saved by the LORD, the shield of your help, and the sword of your triumph!"

8. *Jehovah Elyon* (el-yone') means "The LORD Most High." An example verse is Psalm 7:17, "I will give to the LORD the thanks due to his righteousness, and I will sing praise to the name of the LORD Most High."

9. *Jehovah 'Ezri* (ez-ri) means "The LORD my helper." An example verse is Psalm 30:10, "Hear, O LORD, and be merciful to me! O LORD, be my helper!"

10. *Jehovah Gibbor* (ghib-bore'), in English, means "The LORD the mighty warrior."

    An example verse is Jeremiah 20:11, "But the LORD is with me as a dread warrior; therefore my persecutors will stumble; they will not overcome me."

11. *Jehovah Ga'al* (gaw-al') means "The LORD our redeemer." The example verse for this name is Isaiah 49:26, "Then all flesh shall know that I am the LORD your Savior, and your Redeemer, the Mighty One of Jacob."

12. *Jehovah Hosenu* (ho-say-new), in English, means "The LORD our maker." An example verse is Psalm 95:6, "Oh come, let us worship and bow down; let us kneel before the LORD, our Maker!"

13. *Jehovah Hoshiah* (ho-shi-ya) means "The LORD saves." The example verse is Psalm 20:9, "O LORD, save the king! May he answer us when we call."

14. *Jehovah Jireh* (jee-rah) is "The LORD will provide." An example verse is Genesis 22:14, "So Abraham called the name of that

place, 'The LORD will provide'; as it is said to this day, 'On the mount of the LORD it shall be provided.'"

15. *Jehovah Kanna* (kan-naw') means "The LORD is jealous." An example verse is Exodus 34:14, "For you shall worship no other god, for the LORD, whose name is Jealous, is a jealous God."

16. *Jehovah Keren-Yish'i* (keh'-ren yeh'-shah) means "The LORD the horn of my salvation." The example verse is Psalm 18:2, "The LORD is my rock and my fortress and my deliverer, my God, my rock, in whom I take refuge, my shield, and the horn of my salvation, my stronghold."

17. *Jehovah Machsi* (makh-as-eh') means "The LORD my refuge." This name's example verse is Psalm 91:9, "Because you have made the LORD your dwelling place—the Most High, who is my refuge."

18. *Jehovah Magen* (maw-gawn) is "The LORD my shield." The example verse is Psalm 3:3, "But you, O LORD, are a shield about me, my glory, and the lifter of my head."

19. *Jehovah Mekoddishkem* (me-qo-deesh-kim) is "The LORD who sanctifies you." The example verse is Exodus 31:13, "You are to speak to the people of Israel and say, 'Above all you shall keep my Sabbaths, for this is a sign between me and you throughout your generations, that you may know that I, the LORD, sanctify you.'"

20. *Jehovah Metsudh* (maw-tsood'), in English, is "The LORD my fortress." The example verse is Psalm 18:2, "The LORD is my rock and my fortress and my deliver, my God, my rock, in whom I take refuge, my shield, and the horn of my salvation, my stronghold."

21. *Jehovah Misqab* (miś-gāḇ) is "The LORD my high tower." Psalm 18:2 also provides an example of this name. "The LORD is my

rock and my fortress and my deliverer, my God, my rock, in whom I take refuge, my shield, and the horn of my salvation, my high tower."

22. *Jehovah Nakeh* (naw-kaw') means "The LORD who strikes" in English. The example verse is Ezekiel 7:9, "And my eye will not spare, nor will I have pity. I will punish you according to your ways, while your abominations are in your midst. Then you will know that I am the LORD who strikes."

23. *Jehovah Nekamot* (nek-aw-maw') is translated as "The LORD of vengeance." An example verse is Psalm 94:1, "O LORD, God of vengeance, O God of vengeance, shine forth!"

24. *Jehovah Nissi* (nis-see') is the "The LORD is my banner." An example verse is Exodus 17:15, "And Moses built an altar and called the name of it, 'The LORD is my banner.'"

25. *Jehovah 'Ori* (o-ree) is "The LORD my light." The example verse is Psalm 27:1, "The LORD is my light and my salvation; whom shall I fear? The LORD is the stronghold of my life; of whom shall I be afraid?"

26. *Jehovah Qadosh* (kaw-dosh) is "The Holy One" in English. The example verse is Isaiah 40:25, "To whom then will you compare me, that I should be like him? says the Holy One."

27. *Jehovah Raah* (raw-aw') is translated as "The LORD my shepherd" in English. An example verse is Psalm 23:1, "The LORD is my shepherd; I shall not want."

28. *Jehovah Rapha* (raw-faw') is translated as "The LORD who heals." An example verse is Exodus, "Saying, 'If you will diligently listen to the voice of the LORD your God, and do that which is right in his eyes, and give ear to his commandments and keep all his statutes, I will put none of the diseases on you that I put on the Egyptians, for I am the LORD, your healer.'"

29. *Jehovah Sabaoth* (tsaw-baw') means "The LORD of hosts" or "the LORD of armies." The example verse is 1 Samuel 1:3, "Now this man used to go up year by year from his city to worship and to sacrifice to the LORD of hosts at Shiloh, where the two sons of Eli, Hophni and Phinehas, were priests of the LORD."

30. *Jehovah Selah* (seh'-lah) is "The LORD my rock" in English versions. An example is found in Psalm 18:2, "The LORD is my rock and my fortress and my deliverer, my God, my rock, in whom I take refuge, my shield, and the horn of my salvation, my stronghold."

31. *Jehovah Shalom* (shaw-lome) is "The LORD is peace." An example verse is Judges 6:24, "Then Gideon built an altar there to the LORD and called it, 'The LORD is peace'. To this day it still stands at Ophrah, which belongs to the Abiezrites."

32. *Jehovah Shammah* (shawm-ah) is translated "The LORD is there." The example verse is Ezekiel 48:35, "The circumference of the city shall be 18,000 cubits. And the name of the city from that time on shall be, 'The LORD is there.'"

33. *Jehovah Shaphat* (shaw-fat') means "The LORD the judge." The example verse is Judges 11:27, "I, therefore, have not sinned against you, and you do me wrong by making war on me. The LORD, the Judge, decide this day between the people of Israel and the people of Ammon."

34. Finally, *Jehovah Tsidkenu* (tseh'-dek-in-oo) is translated as "The LORD our righteousness." An example verse is Jeremiah 23:6, "In his days Judah will be saved, and Israel will dwell securely. And this is the name by which he will be called: 'The LORD is our righteousness.'"

Lesson Application - Write down the name of God the Father that resonated with you the most, and do your best to explain why.

Lesson 5

The Son

Context

The previous lesson explored thirty-four different names in the Bible that represent God the Father, the first person of the Trinity. This lesson will explore thirty-three names and titles of the Trinity's second person, the Son. The various biblical names demonstrate that a single name or phrase cannot fully define God. God is more extensive than we can imagine, which is another way we can trust the Bible.

Let's summarize why trusting the Bible is important by looking at three choices people make. The first choice all people have is whether God exists or not. If a person believes God exists, the second choice the person makes is whether Jesus was the incarnate God who came into this world to offer a means of salvation from eternal death. Once a person accepts Jesus, the third choice is to trust the document that reveals God.

Trusting the Bible is important because it is the only document written by God, making it the only physical source of truth in this world. Gaining a better understanding of the Bible's author deepens a believer's faith and trust in God.

The Son

Jesus is the common name of the Trinity's second person, the Son. While the name Jesus is used extensively throughout the New Testament, He is found in Old Testament Scripture. Lesson 3 has a lengthy discussion on the presence of Jesus in the Old Testament, which I'll briefly summarize.

Old Testament passages that contain the angel of the LORD are Christophanies, or the presence of pre-incarnate Jesus. Exodus 3:1-6 provides evidence that the angel of the LORD was the pre-incarnate Jesus, the second person of the Trinity. Here is the passage:

> [1] Now Moses was keeping the flock of his father-in-law, Jethro, the priest of Midian, and he led his flock to the west side of the wilderness and came to Horeb, the mountain of God. [2] And the angel of the Lord appeared to him in a flame of fire out of the midst of a bush. He looked, and behold, the bush was burning, yet it was not consumed. [3] And Moses said, "I will turn aside to see this great sight, why the bush is not burned." [4] When the LORD saw that he turned aside to see, God called to him out of the bush, "Moses, Moses!" And he said, "Here I am." [5] Then he said, "Do not come near; take your sandals off your feet, for the place on which you are standing is holy ground." [6] And he said, "I am the God of your father, the God of Abraham, the God of Isaac, and the God of Jacob." And Moses hid his face, for he was afraid to look at God.

According to Exodus 3:1-6, the angel of the LORD is also called the LORD, the Covenant God of Abraham, Isaac, and Jacob.

Old Testament passages where the angel of the LORD, or the person we commonly call Jesus, include Genesis 16:7–14 and 22:11–18, Exodus 3:2, Judges 2:1-4, 5:23, 6:11-24, and 13:3-22, 2 Samuel 24:16, 2 Kings 19:35, Zechariah 1:12, 3:1, and 12:8. Other Old Testament passages where the LORD appears as a physical presence include Genesis 18:1–33, Joshua 5:13-15, and Daniel 3:25. These passages are also presentations of pre-incarnate Jesus.

Names and Titles of Jesus

The bulk of this lesson lists the various names and titles of the Son. For each of the following thirty-three underlined names, an explanation of its meaning is provided, along with a passage of scripture where the name can be found.

1. Let's begin with the common name, Jesus: Jesus means savior. He is the Savior who came to rescue humanity from sin and reconcile us to God. "Jesus" is derived from the Greek name "Iesous," which is a transliteration of the Hebrew name "Yeshua" or "Joshua" in English. In Hebrew and Greek, the name means "Yahweh saves" or "Yahweh is salvation." An example verse is Matthew 1:21, "She will bear a son, and you shall call his name Jesus, for he will save his people from their sins."

2. The Son is also known as Lord, the equivalent to the Old Testament's use of "Adonai" or "Lord" or "Master." An example is found in Romans 10:13, "For 'everyone who calls on the name of the Lord will be saved.'"

3. Savior is another title and emphasizes Jesus's role as the one who saves us from sin and death, offering us eternal life through faith in Him. An example verse is Titus 2:13, "Waiting for our blessed hope, the appearing of the glory of our great God and Savior Jesus Christ."

4. Messiah and Christ are the same name in different languages. Both terms mean "anointed one" and refer to the promised Savior and King who was anointed by God to fulfill the Messianic prophecies of the Old Testament. "Messiah" comes from the Hebrew word "mashiach," while "Christ" comes from

the Greek word "christos." The example verse is John 1:41, "He [Andrew] first found his own brother Simon and said to him, 'We have found the Messiah' (which means Christ)."

5. Jesus's giving Himself the name "I Am" is a claim that He is the "Yahweh, Jehovah, or Yehovah," the covenant name of the "I AM WHO I AM" or "the LORD" in all caps found in the Old Testament. An example where Jesus makes this claim is John 8:58, "Jesus said unto them, 'Verily, verily, I say unto you, Before Abraham was, I am.'"

6. The angel of the LORD is the common Old Testament name of pre-incarnate Jesus. The example verse is Exodus 3:2, "And the angel of the Lord appeared to him in a flame of fire out of the midst of a bush. He looked, and behold, the bush was burning, yet it was not consumed."

7. Alpha and Omega is a title emphasizing Jesus's eternal and all-encompassing nature as the beginning and end of all things. The example verse is Revelation 22:13, "I am the Alpha and the Omega, the first and the last, the beginning and the end."

8. Emmanuel means "God with us," emphasizing Jesus's divine nature and His role as the fulfillment of God's promise to be with His people. The example verse is Matthew 1:23, "Behold, the virgin shall conceive and bear a son, and they shall call his name Emmanuel (which means, God with us)."

9. The Lamb of God emphasizes Jesus's sacrificial death and His role as the one who takes away the sins of the world. The example verse is John 1:29, "The next day he saw Jesus coming toward him, and said, 'Behold, the Lamb of God, who takes away the sin of the world!'"

10. Redeemer is a title that emphasizes Jesus's role as the one who pays the price to redeem us from sin and death, offering us freedom and new life. A verse where this title is used is Titus

2:14, "Who gave himself for us to redeem us from all lawlessness and to purify for himself a people for his own possession who are zealous for good works."

11. The Word emphasizes Jesus's role as the communication of God to humanity, revealing the truth about God's nature, will, and plan for humanity. The example verse is John 1:1, "In the beginning was the Word, and the Word was with God, and the Word was God."

12. King of Kings is a title emphasizing Jesus's ultimate authority and sovereignty over all earthly and heavenly powers. The example verse is 1 Timothy 6:15, "He who is the blessed and only Sovereign, the King of kings and Lord of lords."

13. High Priest emphasizes Jesus's role as the one who intercedes for His followers before God. The example verse is Hebrews 4:14-16, "Since then we have a great high priest who has passed through the heavens, Jesus, the Son of God, let us hold fast our confession. For we do not have a high priest who is unable to sympathize with our weaknesses, but one who in every respect has been tempted as we are, yet without sin. Let us then with confidence draw near to the throne of grace, that we may receive mercy and find grace to help in time of need."

14. Son of God emphasizes Jesus's divine nature and unique relationship with God the Father as His one and only begotten Son. The example verse is Matthew 16:16, "Simon Peter replied, 'You are the Christ, the Son of the living God.'"

15. Son of Man emphasizes Jesus's humanity, identifying Him as a representative of mankind who came to serve and give His life as a ransom for many. It also highlights His authority and power as the one who was given dominion and kingship by God in Daniel's prophetic vision (7:3). The example verse is

Mark 10:45, "For even the Son of Man came not to be served but to serve, and to give his life as a ransom for many."

16. Son of David emphasizes Jesus's human nature and His connection to King David's lineage, affirming His role as the promised Messiah who came to save His people. The example verse is Matthew 1:1, "The book of the genealogy of Jesus Christ, the son of David, the son of Abraham."

17. Bread of Life emphasizes Jesus's role as the one who sustains and satisfies us, providing us with spiritual nourishment and eternal life. The example verse is John 6:35, "Jesus said to them, 'I am the bread of life; whoever comes to me shall not hunger, and whoever believes in me shall never thirst.'"

18. Light of the World emphasizes Jesus's role as the one who illuminates sin's darkness and brings humanity hope and salvation. The example verse is John 8:12, "Again Jesus spoke to them, saying, 'I am the light of the world. Whoever follows me will not walk in darkness, but will have the light of life.'"

19. The Good Shepherd is a name that emphasizes Jesus's role as the one who cares for, protects, and guides His followers like a shepherd caring for his flock. The example verse is John 10:14-15, "I am the good shepherd. I know my own and my own know me, just as the Father knows me and I know the Father; and I lay down my life for the sheep."

20. The Way emphasizes Jesus's role as the one who provides the way to God and eternal life through His teachings and His sacrificial death on the cross. An example of the name can be seen in John 14:6, "Jesus said to him, 'I am the way, and the truth, and the life. No one comes to the Father except through me.'"

21. The Truth is another name found in John 14:6, which emphasizes Jesus's role as the embodiment of truth, revealing

God's nature and His plan for humanity. Again, the verse states, "Jesus said to him, 'I am the way, and the truth, and the life. No one comes to the Father except through me.'"

22. The Life emphasizes Jesus's role as the source of true and eternal life, offering us the opportunity to live abundantly and experience the fullness of God's love. The example verse for this name is John 11:25-26, "Jesus said to her, 'I am the resurrection and the life. Whoever believes in me, though he die, yet shall he live, and everyone who lives and believes in me shall never die.'"

23. The Resurrection is another name found in John 11:25-26. The name emphasizes the immense power of God Himself. God created the universe and has power over it, including the power to raise the dead. If God did not have such power, He would not be worthy of our faith and worship. Jesus stating that He is the Resurrection is a way for Him to state He is the Creator God and has the power over life and death.

Isaiah 9:6 is the passage for the next four names for the Trinity's second person, the Son. "For to us a child is born, / to us a son is given; / and the government shall be upon his shoulder, / and his name shall be called / Wonderful Counselor, Mighty God, Everlasting Father, Prince of Peace."

24. Wonderful Counselor emphasizes Jesus's role as the source of wisdom, guidance, and comfort for His followers and His ability to provide solutions to life's problems.

25. Mighty God emphasizes Jesus's divine nature and power and His ability to bring salvation and deliverance to His followers.

26. Everlasting Father emphasizes Jesus's eternal and loving nature, and His role as a compassionate father is to care for, protect, and provide for His followers.

27. Prince of Peace emphasizes Jesus's role as the one who brings reconciliation between God and humanity and offers us the peace [shalom] that surpasses all understanding. This is the last name seen in Isaiah 9:6.

28. Holy One is a name that emphasizes Jesus's purity and perfection and His separation from sin and evil. An example verse is Acts 3:14, "But you denied the Holy and Righteous One, and asked for a murderer to be granted to you."

29. Friend of Sinners emphasizes Jesus's compassion and love for all people, especially those who are considered outcasts or marginalized by society. The example verse is Matthew 11:19, "The Son of Man came eating and drinking, and they say, 'Look at him! A glutton and a drunkard, a friend of tax collectors and sinners!' Yet wisdom is justified by her deeds."

30. The Vine is a name that emphasizes Jesus's role as the source of spiritual nourishment and growth for His followers and the importance of abiding in Him for fruitful living. The example verse is John 15:5, "I am the vine; you are the branches. Whoever abides in me and I in him, he it is that bears much fruit, for apart from me you can do nothing."

31. Mediator emphasizes Jesus's role as the one who reconciles God and humanity and who brings peace and harmony between us. The example verse is 1 Timothy 2:5, "For there is one God, and there is one mediator between God and men, the man Christ Jesus."

32. The Prophet emphasizes Jesus's role as the one who speaks God's truth and reveals His will to His followers. The example verse is Luke 13:33, "Nevertheless, I must go on my way today and tomorrow and the day following, for it cannot be that a prophet should perish away from Jerusalem."

33. Finally, the title Rabbi emphasizes Jesus's role as the one who teaches and instructs His followers in the ways of God. The example verse is John 1:38, "Jesus turned and saw them following and said to them, 'What are you seeking?' And they said to him, 'Rabbi' (which means Teacher), 'where are you staying?'"

Lesson Application - Write down the one name for the Son that resonated with you the most and do your best to explain why.

Lesson 6

The Holy Spirit

Context

The previous two lessons highlighted the names and titles of the Father and Son found in the Bible. This lesson examines thirty-three names and titles associated with the Trinity's third person, the Holy Spirit.

The Bible is so intricately tied to God that I question the faith of a person who claims belief in God but does not fully accept the Bible. To begin, the Bible is the only document written by God. Yes, the sixty-six books that constitute the Bible were penned by at least forty different men. But God convicted and guided the men who wrote those books. Miraculously, He directed the meaning behind the words they penned, allowing the personalities of their writers' voices to appear. This lesson examines the names of God the Spirit, who, according to 2 Timothy 3:16, authored the Bible. The various identities describing God in the Bible reinforce how the Spirit guided forty different and often disparate men to pen the words we read today.

The Holy Spirit is God

The Holy Spirit is the common name for the third person of the Trinity and is used throughout the Bible. Generally, the concept of God as the Holy Spirit is harder to comprehend than the concept of God as Father or Son. The following five verses demonstrate that the Holy Spirit is God, just like the Father and the Son. They are presented in order of appearance.

1. The first verse is Psalm 51:11, which states, "Cast me not away from your presence, and take not your Holy Spirit from me." Psalm 51:11 shows that the Holy Spirit is known to have a relationships with an individual person, in this case, David.

   The second verse shows the Holy Spirit can have a relationship with a group of people. Isaiah 63:11 states, "Then he remembered the days of old, of Moses and his people. Where is he who brought them up out of the sea with the shepherds of his flock? Where is he who put in the midst of them his Holy Spirit."

   The third verse shows the Holy Spirit physically interacting, showing He is more than a spiritual influence. Matthew 1:18 states, "Now the birth of Jesus Christ took place in this way. When his mother Mary had been betrothed to Joseph, before they came together, she was found to be with a child from the Holy Spirit." God's Spirit physically manifested within Mary.

   The fourth verse shows that Jesus believed the Holy Spirit was one member of the Triune God. Matthew 28:19 states, "Go therefore and make disciples of all nations, baptizing them in the name of the Father and of the Son and of the Holy Spirit."

   The final verse of the five samples that show the Holy Spirit is God is Acts 5:3-4, where an apostle equates the Holy Spirit to God. The passage states, "But Peter said, "Ananias, why has

Satan filled your heart to lie to the Holy Spirit and to keep back for yourself part of the proceeds of the land? While it remained unsold, did it not remain your own? And after it was sold, was it not at your disposal? Why is it that you have contrived this deed in your heart? You have not lied to man but to God."

Other Names for the Holy Spirit

The remaining thirty-two names for the Holy Spirit show the alternate name underlined and a scripture passage where the name can be found.

2. In Isaiah 61:1, we find the Holy Spirit referred to as the Spirit of the LORD God. The prophet, "The Spirit of the Lord God is upon me, / because the LORD has anointed me / to bring good news to the poor; / he has sent me to bind up the brokenhearted, / to proclaim liberty to the captives, / and the opening of the prison to those who are bound."

3. In Luke 4:18, Jesus quoted the passage from Isaiah but shortened the name to the Spirit of the Lord. Here's Jesus's quote, "The Spirit of the Lord is upon me, / because he has anointed me / to proclaim good news to the poor. / He has sent me to proclaim liberty to the captives / and recovering of sight to the blind, / to set at liberty those who are oppressed."

4. Genesis 1:2 refers to the Holy Spirit as the Spirit of God. "The earth was without form and void, and darkness was over the face of the deep. And the Spirit of God was hovering over the face of the waters."

5. Matthew 10:19-20, we see the name, the Spirit of the Father, which reinforces the Holy Spirit as one of the three persons of the Trinity. "When they deliver you over, do not be anxious how you are to speak or what you are to say, for what you are to say will be given to you in that hour. For it is not you who speak, but the Spirit of your Father speaking through you."

6. In Galatians 4:6, we see the name the Spirit of the Son, the second person of the Trinity. "And because you are sons, God has sent the Spirit of his Son into our hearts, crying, 'Abba! Father!'"

7. The Son is Jesus Christ. First Peter 1:10-11 is a passage where the Holy Spirit is called the Spirit of Christ. "Concerning this salvation, the prophets who prophesied about the grace that was to be yours searched and inquired carefully, 11 inquiring what person or time the Spirit of Christ in them was indicating when he predicted the sufferings of Christ and the subsequent glories."

8. In Job 33:4, we see the Holy Spirit called the Breath of the Almighty. The name can be found: "The Spirit of God has made me, / and the breath of the Almighty gives me life." The Breath of the Almighty was the last action in creating the first man. Genesis 2:7 states, "Then the LORD God formed the man of dust from the ground and breathed into his nostrils the breath of life, and the man became a living creature." Another verse from Genesis, Chapter 7:15, explains that all living creatures rely on God's Spirit, the Breath of the Almighty, for life. "They went into the ark with Noah, two and two of all flesh in which there was the breath of life."

9. Romans 8:2 explains the Spirit of Life as the one who frees us from eternal death. The verse states, "For the law of the Spirit of life has set you free in Christ Jesus from the law of sin and death."

10. The Holy Spirit offers eternal life through Jesus as an act of grace. Hebrews 10:29-31 discusses the consequences of rejecting the Spirit of Grace. "How much worse punishment, do you think, will be deserved by the one who has trampled underfoot the Son of God, and has profaned the blood of the covenant by which he was sanctified, and has outraged the

Spirit of grace? For we know him who said, 'Vengeance is mine; I will repay.' And again, 'The Lord will judge his people.' It is a fearful thing to fall into the hands of the living God."

11. Depending on the translation, John 14:16 refers to the Holy Spirit as <u>Helper</u>, <u>Comforter</u>, <u>Counselor</u>, or <u>Advocate</u>. "And I will ask the Father, and he will give you another Helper, to be with you forever." Later, in verse 26, Jesus adds, "But the Helper, the Holy Spirit, whom the Father will send in my name, he will teach you all things and bring to your remembrance all that I have said to you."

12. <u>Good Spirit</u> is a name in the Old Testament that roughly equates to Jesus's description of the Holy Spirit in John 14:16. Two verses use this name, Nehemiah 9:20, "You gave your good Spirit to instruct them and did not withhold your manna from their mouth and gave them water for their thirst." The second is Psalms 143:10, "Teach me to do your will, / for you are my God! / Let your good Spirit lead me / on level ground!"

13. <u>The Eternal Spirit</u> is who empowered the ministry of Jesus. That name is found in Hebrews 9:13-14, "For if the blood of goats and bulls, and the sprinkling of defiled persons with the ashes of a heifer, sanctify for the purification of the flesh, 14 how much more will the blood of Christ, who through the eternal Spirit offered himself without blemish to God, purify our conscience from dead works to serve the living God."

14. Luke 1:35 uses the name <u>the Power of the Most High</u> or <u>the Power of the Highest</u>. This name equates the Holy Spirit to a member of the Trinity because only God has that power. "And the angel answered her, 'The Holy Spirit will come upon you, and the power of the Most High will overshadow you; therefore the child to be born will be called holy—the Son of God.'"

15. Revelation 19:10 gives us the name the Spirit of Prophecy. It states, "Then I fell down at his feet to worship him, but he said to me, 'You must not do that! I am a fellow servant with you and your brothers who hold to the testimony of Jesus. Worship God.' For the testimony of Jesus is the spirit of prophecy." This name means that all OT prophecy and NT preaching focus on the gospel of the Lord Jesus Christ.

Seven Spirits

16. Revelation 1:4 contains a unique name for the Holy Spirit, the Seven Spirits of God. The complete verse is, "John to the seven churches that are in Asia: / Grace to you and peace from him who is and who was and who is to come, and from the seven spirits who are before his throne."

    One explanation for the Apostle John's use of the Seven Spirits of God is to show the fullness of the Holy Spirit because the number seven represents completeness.

    Another explanation is that the name references the sevenfold ministry of the Holy Spirit through the Messiah, Jesus, prophesied in Isaiah 11:2. In Isaiah 11:2, we see seven names for the Holy Spirit (#17-23). "And the Spirit of the Lord shall rest upon him, / the Spirit of wisdom and understanding, / the Spirit of counsel and might, / the Spirit of knowledge and the fear of the Lord."

17. Thus, the first of the Holy Spirit's sevenfold ministry with the Messiah is to rest upon him. To rest upon the Messiah means the supernatural union is long-term; the Spirit has no plans of leaving. A similar union was God's Spirit staying with David from his anointment in 1 Samuel 16:13 to his death in 1 Kings 2:10.

18. While resting upon the Messiah, the Holy Spirit imparts the five spiritual qualities of Wisdom,

19. Understanding,

20. Counsel,

21. Might, and

22. Knowledge, which all characterize Jesus's ministry, as captured in the Gospels. These blessings will continue to characterize Jesus when He returns to rule the world with a rod of iron, according to Revelation 19:15.

23. The last of the Holy Spirit's blessings upon the Messiah is the Spirit of the Fear of the Lord, demonstrated by Jesus when He stated, "I have not spoken on my own authority, but the Father who sent me has himself given me a commandment—what to say and what to speak," in John 12:40.

24. Psalms 51:12 uses the name Willing or Free Spirit, depending on your translation. "Restore to me the joy of your salvation, / and uphold me with a willing spirit."

25. In Romans 8:15, we see the name Spirit of Adoption. "For you did not receive the spirit of slavery to fall back into fear, but you have received the Spirit of adoption as sons, by whom we cry, 'Abba! Father!'"

26. Spirit of Truth is found in John 14:17. "even the Spirit of truth, whom the world cannot receive, because it neither sees him nor knows him. You know him, for he dwells with you and will be in you."

27. Spirit of Holiness is found in Romans 1:4. "and was declared to be the Son of God in power according to the Spirit of holiness by his resurrection from the dead, Jesus Christ our Lord,"

28. In Ephesians 1:17, we see the name Spirit of Revelation. "that the God of our Lord Jesus Christ, the Father of glory, may give you the Spirit of wisdom and of revelation in the knowledge of him,"

29. Spirit of Judgment is found in Isaiah 4:4. "When the Lord shall have washed away the filth of the daughters of Zion and cleansed the bloodstains of Jerusalem from its midst by a spirit of judgment and by a spirit of burning."

30. Spirit of Burning is another name for the Holy Spirit in Isaiah 4:4, reference above.

31. Isaiah 28:6 uses the name Spirit of Justice. "And a spirit of justice to him who sits in judgment, / and strength to those who turn back the battle at the gate."

32. In 1 Peter 4:14, we see the name Spirit of Glory. "If you are insulted for the name of Christ, you are blessed, because the Spirit of glory and of God rests upon you."

33. Sometimes, the Bible refers to the third person of the Trinity as simply the Spirit. An example is Matthew 4:1, which states, "Then Jesus was led up by the Spirit into the wilderness to be tempted by the devil."

Lesson Application - Write down the one name associated with the Holy Spirit that resonated with you the most, and do your best to explain why.

Lesson 7

God Created Man, Genesis 1

Context

The previous four lessons explored the Trinity: the Father, the Son, and the Holy Spirit. Improving our understanding of God's identity provides at least two benefits; the first is humility, because God is much bigger and more complex than we can fully comprehend. The second benefit is knowing God has authored a document we call the Bible to assist us in living the life He has given us.

In Lesson 2, we examined the different genres of the Bible's books, which include historical pieces, narrative stories, poetry, parables, prophecy, sermons, wisdom literature, gospels, letters, epistles, and apocalyptic literature. Because those stylistically different books are accounts of connected events, narrative is the proper literary term for the overall collection of sixty-six books we call the Bible.

Story is the common, non-literary term for narrative, and story is a fitting term for considering the overall purpose of the Bible. The Bible's overarching story—the narrative that connects all sixty-six books together—is the creation, fall, and redemption of mankind. The Bible's first two chapters contain separate versions of man's creation. This lesson examines the first version, which is found in Genesis 1.

Genesis 1:1

The first sentence of Genesis 1 states, "In the beginning, God created the heavens and the earth." Before moving on to the rest of the chapter's story, let's take a moment to unpack that sentence. The first phrase of the sentence, "In the beginning," is the starting point for the Bible's overarching story.

The sentence's second phrase, "God created," lets us know who initiated the story and how He initiated it. The sentence's last phrase, "the heavens and the earth," is the story's setting. Taken together, the three phrases of the Bible's opening sentence let readers know when the story began, who started the story, and the setting where the story takes place.

Genesis 1:1 contains some truths about the story's first character, God, that should be understood before moving on to the remainder of the story. The first truth is that, because God initiated the story, He must have existed before the story began. This tells us that God is not subject to the same time considerations and constraints inextricably tied to the story's setting. In other words, because He created time, He is outside of and unaffected by time.

The second truth stems from His creation of the story's setting. Because He created the setting, He is not subject to the forces that control the heavens and the earth, such as gravity, friction, and electromagnetism. Furthermore, because He created everything in the setting, He is the rightful owner of everything contained within it. This includes man-made objects that would not exist without the basic building blocks initially created by God.

Thus, when we see God in the Bible's story, we should remember that He is different from all other characters. He is not constrained by time or physical forces, and because He created the setting, He can manipulate everything in it.

How God created the story's setting could be even more interesting. Before He created "the heavens and the earth" in Genesis 1:1, there was no physical matter. Psalm 33:6 and Hebrews 11:3 state that God spoke the world into existence. We see God speaking the world into existence in Genesis 1:3-24, where the phrase, "and God said," is stated seven times before objects or living creatures are added to the story's setting.

Genesis 1:26

Genesis 1:26 opens with the phrase, "Then God said." Up to this point in the creation story, God had filled the heavens and the earth over a period of six days. He has established the story's setting using the phrase "and God said"; the grammatical change to "*then* God said" signifies a deviation in the creation story.

The difference is that God is about to complete the story's setting by adding mankind, the creature for whom the entire Bible exists. Genesis 1:26 reads, "Then God said, 'Let us make man in our image, after our likeness. And let them have dominion over the fish of the sea and over the birds of the heavens and over the livestock and over all the earth and over every creeping thing that creeps on the earth.'"

The second phrase of verse 26, "Let us make man," is informative. The "us" indicates that God sees Himself as more than one person. He adds that man will be made "in our image," which tells us that man is unique because no other creature in the creation story is made in God's image. Thus, the "us" cannot mean the other creatures that populate the earth.

Some have claimed that the "us" represents angels, but like the animals, angels do not bear the image of God. We know this from Genesis 3:1, which states, "Now the serpent was more crafty than any other beast of the field that the Lord God had made."

This verse shows us that the serpent—who is the fallen angel, Satan—is a beast just like the other animals created in Genesis 1.

Another explanation for God's use of "us" in Genesis 1:26 is that He is using language that indicates the plurality of His majesty. In other words, He is using "the royal we." While this explanation is possible, the remainder of the Bible provides very little—if any—evidence that God refers to Himself in the same way human beings refer to themselves as a plural entity. In fact, in Exodus 3:14, after Moses asks for God's name, God tells him that His name is "I AM." God does not add lofty or exalted pontifications to His name. He provides Moses with a straightforward name that would be impossible to misinterpret for someone else. The simplicity of the name He gives to Moses is that He exists.

So, when God states, "Let us make man in our image" in Genesis 1:26, He cannot mean the image of other creatures, including angels, and it is highly unlikely that He is referring to Himself in a majestic plurality. Christian theologians believe this is one of the references to the Holy Trinity, the three separate persons of God. In Matthew 28:19, Jesus distinguishes those persons as the Father, the Son, and the Holy Spirit.

We Bear God's Image

Let's delve into what it means to bear God's image. Obviously, mankind reflects God through intellect, emotions, will, creativity, and language. Mankind is driven to classify things and believes in basic dignity and inherent significance in living things. Mankind is relational in nature. People seek purpose in their lives and know right from wrong.

What truly separates mankind from the other living creatures God created is a person's ability to choose. While physical needs must be met, mankind has a level of choice that other living creatures—such as beasts—do not have. Beasts do what God created them to do and live within the parameters and instincts God placed inside them. For example, dogs always behave like dogs. Birds do bird things, and fish do fish things. Each image-bearer has the fundamental choice to accept or reject God. Furthermore, image-bearers can live righteously or choose to live contrary to God's will.

These image-bearing characteristics (intellect, will, language, choice, etc.) are non-physical attributes. They are metaphysical and supernatural, speaking to our true selves. In other words, if you were to describe a person without using any physical traits, our image-bearing qualities are what you would use. For example, you might describe someone as being smart, kind, loving, wild, quiet, nurturing, or antagonistic. This leads to the following observation about what it means to bear God's image.

We have a spiritual self that is separate from our physical self. Our spiritual self, often called the soul, is what bears God's image. Our current physical bodies do not bear God's image because they are temporary and will die in this world that God created; however, our souls live forever. Ecclesiastes 12:7, Daniel 12:2, and 2 Corinthians 5:8 are a few verses that tell us our souls are immortal.

In Matthew 25:46, Jesus said the dead either go "away to eternal punishment" or "eternal life." In other words, when our bodies die, our image-bearing souls will either reside with God in heaven or be sent to a place called hell. As Christians, we know the only way to reside with God the Father in heaven is to accept His Son, Jesus, as Lord and Savior, which leads to receiving God's Holy Spirit. As image-bearers, we can choose an eternal relationship with our Creator or an eternity without our Creator.

When a person receives the Holy Spirit, the person produces the spiritual fruit listed in Galatians 5:22-23: "...love, joy, peace, patience, kindness, goodness, faithfulness, gentleness, and self-control." The receipt of God's Spirit is why choice separates mankind from other living creatures. While the previously mentioned image-bearing characteristics are true, the most essential aspect of bearing God's image is simply choosing to accept God for who He says He is.

The second sentence of Genesis 1:26 states, "And let them have dominion over the fish of the sea and over the birds of the heavens and over the livestock and over all the earth and over every creeping thing that creeps on the earth." God giving mankind dominion over the earth is an extension of man's image-bearing duties. Having dominion over the fish, birds, livestock, and every creeping thing allows man to model and extend God's care for those living creatures and reflect God's spiritual fruit to the rest of creation in service to His will.

Male and Female

Genesis 1:27 reads, "So God created man in his own image, / in the image of God he created him; / male and female he created them." Biblical experts universally understand this verse to mean mankind is divided into two types: male and female. Thus, men and women are equal because both bear God's image.

It is clear that men and women are different. They are physically different and generally have different abilities, desires, and responses to the world's stimuli. While men and women are different, they bear God's image equally to the rest of creation. A way to think about this is that men and women are two sides of the same coin. Only when the two images are printed on the same coin does the coin's value become fully realized. A man and woman together—who both choose righteousness—will reflect God's nature better than a separate individual.

Verse 28 states, "And God blessed them. And God said to them, 'Be fruitful and multiply and fill the earth and subdue it, and have dominion over the fish of the sea and over the birds of the heavens and over every living thing that moves on the earth.'"

This is the second blessing in Genesis 1. The first blessing is found in verse 22 where God blesses the fish and birds He created so they would "Be fruitful and multiply." In other words, God's blessing upon man—male and female—has to do with procreation, their ability to reproduce to "multiply and fill the earth."

He also charges mankind with subduing the earth to provide a secure environment for other living creatures. He gave mankind dominion over the other creatures to assist mankind in subduing and establishing a secure environment for His creation. God did not create mankind to be equal to the other living creatures. Image bearers have God-ordained authority over the other living creatures to ensure that God's blessing of fruitfulness and multiplication occur.

Summary

Genesis 1 establishes many truths about the biblical story. The opening verse lets readers know when the story began, who started the story, and the setting where the story will take place. Because God created time, He is outside of and unaffected by it. From nothing, God spoke this world into existence. Seven times in Genesis 1:3-25 we are told, "And God said," and one time, "Then God said" (v. 26). Because He created the setting, He is not subject to the natural laws controlling the heavens and the earth such as gravity, friction, and electromagnetism. He is the rightful owner of everything the setting contains.

From the verses where God created mankind, we know that God sees Himself as more than one person (v. 26). Man is uniquely made in God's image (v. 26). Man has an immortal soul and can choose his eternity (v. 26). Both the male and female versions of man are image-bearers (v. 27). God blessed both male and female versions to "be fruitful and multiply" and tasked both with subduing the story's setting of the earth and having dominion over it (v. 28).

Lesson Application - Write down one of the truths found in the opening chapter of the Bible that resonated with you and explain why it resonated.

Lesson 8

God Created Man, Genesis 2

Context

In the last lesson, we examined the Genesis 1 version of mankind's creation. A summary of Genesis 1 is that God created the male and female versions of mankind to be equal—equal in bearing His image and equal in multiplying and subduing His creation.

This lesson examines the chapter-two version of the creation of mankind. Genesis 2 differs from Genesis 1 in that it discusses specific tasks God gave to the male version of mankind and how the female version complements those tasks.

Genesis 2

Chapter two opens by relating how God rested on the seventh day following the six days of creation. The second version of man's creation begins in Genesis 2:7 and states, "Then the LORD God formed the man of dust from the ground and breathed into his nostrils the breath of life, and the man became a living creature."

Interestingly, Genesis 2 is when the name "the LORD God" is used for the first time. Referring to God as "the LORD" is not seen in chapter one. Chapter one only uses the name "God." Genesis 2:4 is the first time we see the name "the LORD God," and its use in verse seven is the third time it is used.

Lesson 4 provides a more comprehensive discussion on the significance of the name "the LORD." To summarize that discussion, when we see the Bible's use of "the LORD" in all capital letters, we should understand this is God's covenant name—the "I AM" found in Exodus 3:14. It is written as YHWH in Hebrew and pronounced as Yahweh or Jehovah. The single name "God" in Hebrew is Elohim.

Verse seven tells us that the LORD God—or Yahweh Elohim in Hebrew—"formed the man of dust from the ground" then "breathed into his nostrils the breath of life" and the "man [became] a living creature." God's first action was to form the man from dust, then breathed life into the man's nostrils, bringing him to life. Genesis 3:19 confirms this beginning when God tells Adam, "You are dust, and to dust you shall return."

Verse eight states, "And the LORD God planted a garden in Eden, in the east, and there he put the man whom he had formed." So, after God formed man from dust and breathed life into him, God placed man in a garden He planted in a land He called Eden. Apparently, Eden is located to the east of where God made man. Notice the garden is not *called* Eden; the garden is located *in* Eden.

Verse nine tells us about the trees in the garden. It states, "And out of the ground the Lord God made to spring up every tree that is pleasant to the sight and good for food. The tree of life was in the midst of the garden, and the tree of the knowledge of good and evil." The trees that God sprung up are described as "pleasant to the sight and good for food." The verse also contains two unique trees: "...the tree of life and the tree of the knowledge of good and evil."

Verses ten to fourteen describe a river that flowed out of the garden and became four separate rivers. Since two of the rivers, the Tigris and Euphrates, are named for rivers today, many believe the garden in

Eden must have been located somewhere in the Middle East, where the current rivers are located. The worldwide flood described in Genesis 7, however, likely changed the entire geography of the world. Thus, the current Tigris and Euphrates Rivers are unlikely to be the same ones named in Genesis 2.

God's Four Tasks for Men

God gave man four tasks after placing him in the garden in Eden. As men, we need to understand the four tasks because they still apply to us today; God's tasks to men have not changed. The four tasks are contained in Genesis 2:15-23. The first two tasks are found in verse fifteen, which states: "The LORD God took the man and put him in the garden of Eden to work it and keep it." God's first two tasks to man were to work and keep the garden.

To work a garden means tending, caring for, and nurturing individual plants for maximum growth; it includes reaping the ripened fruit so the plant can produce more fruit. To work or tend a garden is to produce as much fruit as possible through focused care on individual plants. It also means caring for the garden's creatures and ensuring they have what they need. Think of an ecosystem where all living things—plants and animals—coexist in the same environment and depend on one another for continued existence. Synonyms for *working* include tending, cultivating, watering, feeding, planting, shearing, maintaining, managing, ministering to, nurturing, and nursing.

To keep a garden means to guard, watch over, and protect all of the garden's fruit-producing plants. Keeping implies the man does not own the garden. The man cannot give or sell God's garden. Since man's first task was to work, tend, and care for God's garden, protecting or keeping the garden was necessary. Synonyms for keeping include conserving, guarding, holding, preserving, protecting, retaining, and saving.

Verses sixteen and seventeen provide the third task God gave to man after He placed him in the garden: obeying God's command. The verses state, "And the LORD God commanded the man, saying, 'You may surely eat of every tree of the garden, but of the tree of the knowledge of good and evil you shall not eat, for in the day that you eat of it you shall surely die.'"

God tells man that he can eat from any of the trees, which verse nine describes as "pleasant to the sight and good for food." Think of all the different kinds of fruit we have today. I don't know if the man had the same kinds of fruit or not, but we can safely assume the man had a wide variety of good fruit to eat. Then God commanded him not to eat the fruit from one of the two unique trees—the "tree of the knowledge of good and evil." God elaborates on the command by telling the man that when—not *if*—the man eats from the tree of the knowledge of good and evil, he will "surely die."

Until this point in the creation story, the only person in the garden is the male version of mankind. Verses eighteen to twenty-three add the female version and provide the fourth of the four tasks God gave to man. Those verses state:

> [18] Then the Lord God said, "It is not good that the man should be alone; I will make him a helper fit for him." [19] Now out of the ground the Lord God had formed every beast of the field and every bird of the heavens and brought them to the man to see what he would call them. And whatever the man called every living creature, that was its name. [20] The man gave names to all livestock and to the birds of the heavens and to every beast of the field. But for Adam there was not found a helper fit for him. [21] So the Lord God caused a deep sleep to fall upon the man, and while he slept took one of his ribs and closed up its place with flesh. [22] And the rib that the Lord God had taken from the man he made into a woman and brought her to the man. [23] Then the man said, / "This at last is bone of my bones

/ and flesh of my flesh; / she shall be called Woman, / because she was taken out of Man."

In verse twenty of the passage, the man named the animals God had previously created in Genesis 1:20-25. And in verse twenty-three, the man named the helper whom God created for him; thus, the fourth task God gave to man was to name the other creatures He created. By naming the other creatures, man exercised his authority over the other creatures. Naming is an exercise of authority because it establishes identity.

When taken together, the four tasks God gave to man in the order they were given were: to tend, to keep, to obey, and to name. The LORD God tasked the man in the garden that He had planted. The garden was not man's garden; it was God's garden. This tells us about man's position in relation to God. Using current terminology, we could say that the man supervised or managed God's garden. Using a common biblical term, the man was the steward of God's garden in Eden.

Furthermore, God did not ask the man if he wanted to steward His garden. God does not seem concerned about the man's desires but recognizes that a helper was necessary for the man. Therefore, God planted a garden, placed the man in it, and gave instructions on how to properly tend the garden before providing His steward with a helper.

Our current position with God is no different. God has placed us over a portion of His creation and tasked us with proper stewardship of it. Most men have a woman who could also assist them in their God-given tasks. Let's discuss her inclusion in the second creation story.

There are two verses in Genesis 2 when God discusses the man's need for a helper. Verse eighteen states, "Then the LORD God said, 'It is not good that the man should be alone; I will make him a helper fit for him.'" And in verse twenty, as Adam is naming the animals, we find this sentence, "But for Adam there was not found a helper fit for him."

We can safely assume that while Adam was naming the animals, he noticed that no other creature was like him. He had to have recognized that among the living creatures, he was uniquely alone.

In verses twenty-one and twenty-two, God creates a woman from the man. In verse twenty-three, the man names the woman. The English word *woman* means "to come from man." This is no different from the original Hebrew, where the name for man is "Ish" and the name for woman is "Ish'a," which also means "to come from man."

Summary of the Creation Stories

Ten distinct events sequence the second creation story in Genesis 2.

1. God creates a man in verse seven.
2. God plants a garden in verse eight.
3. God places the man in the garden in verses eight and fifteen.
4. God tasks the man to tend the garden in verse fifteen.
5. God tasks the man to keep the garden, also in verse fifteen.
6. God commands the man not to eat the fruit from one tree in verses sixteen & seventeen.
7. God says the man needs a helper fit for him in verse eighteen.
8. God tasks the man to name the other creatures, verses nineteen & twenty.
9. God says a second time that the man needs a helper fit for him in verse twenty.
10. God creates a woman from the man in verses twenty-one to twenty-three.

Based on the ten events in Genesis 2, it is evident that God created the man to steward the garden He planted. God created the woman to help the man with his stewardship responsibilities.

In Genesis 1, which is the first creation story, we see that men and women bear God's image and likeness equally. Additionally, God blessed and tasked them with multiplying and subduing His creation.

The second creation story in Genesis 2 shows God assigning man and woman with different roles in multiplying and subduing His creation. God made man the responsible party, which the Bible commonly refers to as stewardship. The woman was created to help man steward God's creation.

Men, just because the creation stories occurred a long time ago does not mean our responsibility for stewarding God's creation is any different. In Malachi 3:6, God declared, "For I the Lord do not change." Revelation 1:8 states, "I am the Alpha and the Omega,' says the Lord God, 'who is and who was and who is to come, the Almighty.'" Both Malachi 3:6 and Revelation 1:8 state that God has not changed and never will change; therefore, His commands and will remain unchanged.

The placement of man as the steward of creation and the woman as man's helper has not changed. Hebrews 13:8-9 explains why. "Jesus Christ is the same yesterday and today and forever. Do not be led away by diverse and strange teachings." Our culture has rightly taught that men and women are equal. Genesis 1 shows us how we are equal. Our culture has mistakenly taught that men and women have no differences. According to Genesis 2, we were created for different roles and responsibilities. Men are the stewards of God's creation, and women were created to help men fulfill their roles and responsibilities.

Lesson Application – Select one of the four tasks God gives to His stewards (tend, keep, name/exercise authority, and obey) and explain why a man in our current society may have difficulties in accomplishing the task.

Lesson 9

A Servant's Heart

Obedience Is a Choice

The previous two lessons examined how God created man and woman to be equal but different. Genesis 1 tells us that man and woman bear God's image equally, and both were blessed and commanded to multiply and subdue God's creation. Genesis 2 shows that the man and woman had different responsibilities in subduing creation. God created the man to steward His garden and created the woman to help the man fulfill his stewardship responsibilities. In short, men and women bear God's image equally; each obediently serves in His creation with different roles and responsibilities.

The man and woman were removed from the garden because of their disobedience, but if God wanted man and woman to serve His creation obediently, why did He put the tree of the knowledge of good and evil in a place where they could easily eat its fruit?

The answer is that mankind bears God's image, which is the same answer to the question of why a good or loving God would allow evil. Because we bear God's image, we all have the ability to choose whether to obey God or not. Without choice, mankind would be like all other creatures whose behavior is dictated by the needs, desires, and instincts related to food, water, shelter, and sexual reproduction. Without choice, mankind would be a robot programmed to behave solely out of survival motives. With choice, mankind can live for a higher purpose than self. With choice, mankind can demonstrate love through selfless and obedient service to God.

The Heart Makes Choices

We can localize where choices are made using four verses from the book of Proverbs: Proverbs 3:5 states, "Trust in the LORD with all your heart, and do not lean on your own understanding." Proverbs 16:1 states, "The plans of the heart belong to man, but the answer of the tongue is from the LORD." Proverbs 16:9 states, "The heart of man plans his way, but the LORD establishes his steps." And, Proverbs 21:2 states, "Every way of a man is right in his own eyes, but the LORD weighs the heart."

The problem with the heart making choices is that man's heart is evil. After his affair with Bathsheba came to light, David wrote in Psalm 51:5, "Behold, I was brought forth in iniquity, and in sin did my mother conceive me."

In the failed attempt to prevent the nation of Judah from a Babylonian exile, the prophet Jeremiah preached God's word. In Chapter 17:9, Jeremiah wrote, "The heart is deceitful above all things, and desperately sick; who can understand it?"

During a confrontation with Pharisees who accused Him of not maintaining ritualistic cleansing, Jesus stated in Mark 7:21-23, "For from within, out of the heart of man, come evil thoughts, sexual immorality, theft, murder, adultery, coveting, wickedness, deceit, sensuality, envy, slander, pride, foolishness. All these evil things come from within, and they defile a person." And the evilness of man's heart is not limited to a few people.

The Bible states that no one is good, as indicated in Psalm 14:3, where David wrote, "They have all turned aside; together they have become corrupt; there is none who does good, not even one." Solomon reaches the same conclusion in Ecclesiastes 7:20: "Surely there is not a righteous man on earth who does good and never sins." Paul reiterates the human condition in Romans 3:11-12, "None is righteous, no, not one; no one understands; no one seeks for God. All have turned aside; together they have become worthless; no one does good, not even one." And in verse 23, Paul concludes, "for all have sinned and fall short of the glory of God."

It is safe to say the Bible shows all men are afflicted with a corrupt and wicked heart—the image-bearing part of ourselves—where choices are made. The Apostle Paul explains why God provided the law to all mankind in Galatians 3:24-26, "...the law was our guardian until Christ came, in order that we might be justified by faith. But now that faith has come, we are no longer under a guardian, for in Christ Jesus you are all sons of God, through faith." Faith in Jesus frees a person from the law's standards, but that doesn't mean the law has changed, or does change.

In Matthew 7:12 and Luke 16:16, Jesus refers to the entire Old Testament as the law and prophets. In His Sermon on the Mount, Jesus stated, "Do not think that I have come to abolish the Law or the Prophets; I have not come to abolish them but to fulfill them. For truly, I say to you, until heaven and earth pass away, not an iota, not a dot, will pass from the Law until all is accomplished. Therefore whoever relaxes one of the least of these commandments and teaches others to do the same will be called least in the kingdom of heaven, but whoever does them and teaches them will be called great in the kingdom of heaven. For I tell you, unless your righteousness exceeds that of the scribes and Pharisees, you will never enter the kingdom of heaven" (Matthew 5:17-20).

Righteousness

The people who heard Jesus's Sermon on the Mount understood righteousness from the writings contained in the Law and the Prophets. For example, Proverbs 10:2 states, "Treasures gained by wickedness do not profit, but righteousness delivers from death." The juxtaposition of righteousness against wickedness delineates the two behaviors, helping us to understand what is opposite of righteousness. Righteousness is close to but not equal to goodness.

When approached by the rich young ruler who called Him a "good teacher," Jesus stated in Mark 10:18, "Why do you call me good? No one is good except God alone." If goodness is unattainable to man, it must be because "being good" has something to do with the purity that only exists with God. While we cannot attain goodness, we can be righteous.

Genesis 15:6 provides the clearest explanation for how someone becomes righteous. The verse states Abraham "believed the LORD, and he counted it to him as righteousness." Abraham became righteous because he believed the LORD God would fulfill His promises. In a display of the importance of Abraham's belief in God's promises, three New Testament verses (Romans 4:3, Galatians 6:3, James 2:23) all quote the Genesis 15:6 passage where God counts Abraham as righteous.

Philippians 3:9 further clarifies how a person becomes righteous when Paul states his "righteousness [does not come] from the law, but…comes through faith in Christ." When Jesus gave His Sermon on the Mount, He was telling people the righteousness demanded by God's Law is achieved by faith in Him, the promised Messiah about whom the Prophets wrote.

Titus 3:5-6 explains how righteousness—achieved through faith in Christ—is accomplished. The verse states God "saved us, not because of works done by us in righteousness, but according to his own mercy, by the washing of regeneration and renewal of the Holy Spirit." Righteousness is not *works*; it is having the Holy Spirit dwell in our hearts because of our faith in Jesus Christ.

The Holy Spirit Changes Hearts

In John 14:26, while Jesus was preparing His disciples for His departure, He told them, "But the Helper, the Holy Spirit, whom the Father will send in my name, he will teach you all things and bring to your remembrance all that I have said to you." Following Jesus's ascension to heaven, Acts 2:4 states the disciples "were all filled with the Holy Spirit" during the Pentecost holiday celebration. In 1 Corinthians 6:19, Paul claimed the indwelling Holy Spirit made a believer's body "a temple of the Holy Spirit."

Once we receive the Holy Spirit, our image-bearing qualities change because of the indwelling Holy Spirit. More specifically, the indwelling Holy Spirit transforms our hearts into a temple for God.

About 600 years before Jesus, God told the Old Testament prophet Ezekiel in Chapter 36:26-27 where His Spirit would abide. God stated, "And I will give you a new heart, and a new spirit I will put within you. And I will remove the heart of stone from your flesh and give you a heart of flesh. And I will put my Spirit within you, and cause you to walk in my statutes and be careful to obey my rules." About thirty years after Jesus ascended to heaven, Paul specified where the Spirit dwells in Romans 5:5, which was part of his letter to the Romans. "And hope does not put us to shame, because God's love has been poured into our hearts through the Holy Spirit who has been given to us."

God's Spirit dwells in the hearts of believers in Jesus, transforming their hearts from stone to a living source of life. John 7:37-39 shows what Jesus stated during His final Passover meal. He "stood up and cried out, 'If anyone thirsts, let him come to me and drink. Whoever believes in me, as the Scripture has said, 'Out of his heart will flow rivers of living water.' Now this he said about the Spirit, whom those who believed in him were to receive, for as yet the Spirit had not been given, because Jesus was not yet glorified."

So, as image-bearers, we have the ability to choose whether to live righteously according to God's will or wickedly against His will, but we begin life with wicked hearts that can only be purified by God's Spirit. Believing in Jesus as Lord and Savior allows the Holy Spirit to clean our wicked hearts.

Even after we receive God's cleansing Spirit, we still have the ability to choose to go against God's will and pollute our cleansed hearts. This is why Proverbs 4:23 tells us to "Guard your heart with all vigilance, / for from it flow the springs of life." We must protect where our choices are made because bad choices make a poor servant. So, men, guard your heart so you can serve the God whose image you bear in righteous obedience.

Lesson Application – What can you do to guard your heart and maintain righteousness? Explain how that method can and will guard your heart.

Lesson 10

God's Stewards

Context

The previous lesson ended with an appeal to guard your hearts and keep them pure so you can serve the God whose image you bear in righteous obedience.

Men, our service to God is spelled out in Genesis 2. We are to tend and protect the portion of creation God has placed under our authority while maintaining our obedience to His will. Using a common biblical term, we are God's stewards.

The Logic of Stewardship

There is a logic to why we should think of ourselves as God's stewards. First, we know that God created everything in this physical world, including the atoms, elements, molecules, and compounds man has used and adapted to build technologically advanced societies. God created everything in this world that our physical senses can detect. Whatever we see, hear, smell, touch, and taste originates from God. Examples of God's creation include people, pets, livestock, land, homes, cars, computers, books, bridges, boats, guns, etc. God is the original owner of everything in this world.

Now, let's consider some truths about mankind. According to Jeremiah 1:5, Matthew 10:28, and James 2:26, we are eternal souls who get a temporary body when we enter this physical world. Thus, when our souls enter this world, we arrive with physical bodies that will die. And when our bodies die, our immortal souls will exit this world without taking anything physical from it. Our souls enter this world with nothing and leave with nothing. While we exist in this physical world, God places us in authority over a portion of it.

Since we do not own what God places under our authority, the best way to think of our existence as men is that we are temporary stewards of God's creation. All of us are responsible for a portion of what God has created. When our bodies die, someone else will assume responsibility for what is left of the portion God placed in our care. Meanwhile, our bodiless souls will give an account of our stewardship to our Creator.

Perhaps a more familiar phrasing of this accounting is the Day of Judgment, which is discussed in Matthew 12:36, John 12:48, Romans 14:10, Hebrews 9:27, and Revelation 20:11-15.

Man Will Choose Disobedience

The creation stories in Genesis 1 and 2 are followed by the Fall of Man story in chapter 3. A summary of that story is that the man and woman failed to obey the one command God gave to the man in Genesis 2:16-17, "You may surely eat of every tree of the garden, but of the tree of the knowledge of good and evil you shall not eat, for in the day that you eat of it you shall surely die." In disobedience to God's command, the man and woman ate the tree's fruit, ensuring they would someday die.

A key lesson we can draw from Adam is that obedience to God is central to our stewardship responsibilities, but we begin our stewardship with a problem.

According to Romans 5:12, Adam's disobedience has been passed down to the rest of us, meaning we all have a natural inclination to choose sin over God's will, and that natural desire ensures our death. Meaning, without a supernatural rescue from our natural choices, we are all doomed to fail in our stewardship tasks. Thankfully, the same God who created us also loved us enough to provide the necessary supernatural rescue.

Before I explain God's rescue, I want to emphasize that He never takes away our ability to choose. God is all-powerful and could fix our natural inclination to choose sin at this very moment—but He doesn't. He doesn't force our decisions even when we desperately need to be rescued from them.

The Supernatural Rescue

Our need to be rescued from our natural desire to choose sin is perhaps why John 3:16 is so popular. It states, "For God so loved the world, that he gave his only Son, that whoever believes in him should not perish but have eternal life." Our sin leads to death, but we can choose Jesus and have life. Let's review why Jesus is the supernatural rescue we need to have life.

According to 1 Timothy 2:5 and Hebrews 4:15, Jesus was a man like the rest of us. He was flesh and blood and dealt with the world's temptations to sin. John 1:1 tells us that Jesus was God in the flesh; thus, He could have used His power to destroy the world's sin. But Philippians 2:7-8 tells us that Jesus "humbled himself by becoming obedient to the point of death."

In other words, while Jesus certainly used His deity to heal people and cast out demons, He did not use His power to prevent mankind's ability to choose sin. He maintained obedience to the point of death, but obedience to what? In John 8:28 and 12:49, Jesus told listeners that He only speaks what the Father tells Him to speak.

In other words, the Son maintains obedience to the Father's will at all times. The Garden of Gethsemane scene, described in all four Gospels—Matthew 26:42, Mark 14:36, Luke 22:42, and John 12:27-28—demonstrates Jesus maintaining obedience to the Father even as He faced a brutal death.

Since Jesus maintained obedience to God's will during His existence in this world, Hebrews 10:8-14 tells us that He was the only person who could fulfill the perfect sin sacrifice. First John 2:2 states, "He is the propitiation for our sins, and not for ours only but also for the sins of the whole world." In other words, Jesus paid the price of death for all of the sins committed in the world before and after His death on the cross.

Further, because He was a sinless man, He was the only person who could have paid that price. Jesus's sacrificial death was God's supernatural rescue.

Jesus paying the price of death for our sins offers the opportunity for us to have life. The life Jesus offers is certainly the eternal life He speaks about in Matthew 25:46.

The life Jesus offers also applies to our stewardship responsibilities in this world. Here's a rhetorical question that explains why: Do you think God wants us to successfully steward His creation?

Of course, He wants us to be successful. Genesis 1:31 tells us that when God completed creation and "saw everything that he had made," He saw that "it was very good." God would not want His creation to be anything less than very good.

Here's a non-rhetorical question: Why would an all-powerful and sovereign God make imperfect and prone-to-sin men the stewards of His creation?

The short answer begins with the fact that He loves us, as stated in John 3:16. Second Corinthians 5:21 adds, "For our sake he made him to be sin who knew no sin, so that in him we might become the righteousness of God." In Matthew 5:20, Jesus stated that without righteousness, we "can never enter the kingdom of heaven."

God makes us stewards of His creation and gives us the opportunity to become righteous so we can be in a loving relationship with Him as citizens of the Kingdom of Heaven. In our service as stewards, we have an opportunity to understand the God who created us, thus deepening our respect, admiration, and love for Him. We exercise authority over our portion of God's creation to improve and protect it while maintaining obedience to God's will so we can make good decisions about what He wants for His creation.

When we serve as righteous stewards, we enter into an intimate relationship with God where we begin to receive His insight and wisdom. For example, I did not understand unconditional love until I held my first child, which was a natural understanding of love. God led me to a supernatural understanding that love is a choice, meaning I could choose to unconditionally love other people such as my wife.

Supernatural wisdom comes from God. More specifically, it comes from the Holy Spirit with whom we are baptized when we choose to accept and believe that Jesus died for our sins and conquered death through resurrection. Once we accept Jesus, God—as the Holy Spirit—resides in our hearts and helps us with decision-making capabilities (Ezekiel 36:26-27 and Romans 5:5). The Holy Spirit is how God equips us for righteous stewardship of His creation. With the Holy Spirit guiding our choices and decisions, we can maintain obedience to God's will. Like any other skill, it takes practice to become proficient in allowing God's Spirit to guide our decisions.

What Obedience Allows

Our practice of learning to maintain obedience while stewarding our portion of God's creation is called sanctification. Sanctification deepens our relationship with God.

The longer we practice sanctification, the more we become like Jesus—who was obedient to death.

Reviewing the lessons in the *Discipled Warriors Handbook* is part of your sanctification process because you study the truth and renew your mind. We will someday give an account of our portion of God's creation before our Lord Jesus Christ. To serve God as righteous stewards, we must be obedient to Him. Obedience begins with us choosing Jesus as our Lord and Savior and then choosing to listen to God's Spirit as we tend and keep what God has placed under our authority. Our choice to be obedient improves what we steward and allows us to participate in the Kingdom of God as righteous servants.

This is a good time to consider what God has placed under your authority. Consider what is in your care from the inside and work outward. Start with your mind, heart, soul, and spirit. Whatever you call your non-physical, immortal self, it was created by God and placed under your authority. You control your will, emotions, thoughts, language, choices, etc.

Next is your body. You have stewardship over the temporary body God created for you to exist in this physical world.

How about other image-bearers? Married men are stewards of their wives. Men with families are stewards of their children.

Men are stewards of the work they perform in their jobs, careers, and professions. We are stewards of the place we call home and everything our homes contain. We are stewards of the relationships with other image-bearers. There are likely other portions of creation that men steward.

The point is to be consciously aware of what God has placed under your authority so you will at least know what you will be held accountable for on the Day of Judgment.

Lesson Application - List what God has placed under your authority as His steward. Then, determine whether an area under your authority is a strength or weakness (i.e., S or W). Then, make a note next to the weak areas on how you can strengthen those areas.

Lesson 11

The Enemy

Context

Earlier lessons established the tenet that the Bible is our single source of truth in this world. Lessons then examined who God is and how He created everything. The Bible tells us that men and women are equal in their service to God's creation, but have different roles and responsibilities.

Our biggest hurdle as God's servants is our hearts' desire for disobedience. The natural heart is selfishly evil, but out of His love for us, God offered Jesus as the only sacrifice worthy of washing away our sins. Those who believe in Jesus as Lord and Savior are gifted with the Holy Spirit who dwells in their hearts, transforming them into a potential source of good decisions.

The next problem we have in obediently serving God is that we have an active enemy who wants to destroy God's creation. We often call our enemy Satan, or the devil, but he has over thirty names in the Bible, spanning nine OT books and twenty-one NT books.

Names for the enemy in alphabetical order include: Abaddon - Rev 9:11; Accuser of our brothers - Rev 12:10; Adversary - 1 Pet 5:8; Angel of the bottomless pit - Rev 9:11; Angels who sinned - 2 Pet 2:4; Apollyon - Rev 9:11; Beelzebub or Beelzebul - Matt 12:24; Belial - 2

Cor 6:15; Devil - Heb 2:14; Distressing spirit - 1 Sam 16:14; Dragon - Rev 20:2; Enemy - Matt 13:39; Father of lies - John 8:44; Fleeing serpent - Is 27:1; Great red dragon - Rev 12:3; Leviathan - Is 27:1; Liar - John 8:44; Lying spirit - 1 Kings 22:22; Murderer - John 8:44; Prince of the power of the air - Eph 2:2; Reptile - Is 27:1; Ruler of the darkness of this world - Eph 6:12; Ruler of the demons - Matt 12:24; Ruler of this world - John 14:30; Satan - 1 Chr 21:1; Serpent - Gen 3:4; Serpent of old - Rev 12:9; Spirit who works in the sons of disobedience - Eph 2:2; Tempter - Matt 4:3; The god of this age - 2 Cor 4:4; Twisted serpent - Is 27:1; and, Wicked one - Matt 13:19. As those thirty-two names demonstrate, the enemy is located throughout the biblical story.

The Bible's Villain

The first place we see the enemy in the Bible follows the creation stories in Genesis 1 and 2. Genesis 3:1 states, "Now the serpent was more crafty than any other beast of the field that the LORD God had made. He said to the woman, 'Did God actually say, "You shall not eat of any tree in the garden"?'"

The serpent is Satan or the devil. The Apostle John confirms the serpent is the enemy in Revelation 12:9, which states, "And the great dragon was thrown down, that ancient serpent, who is called the devil and Satan, the deceiver of the whole world—he was thrown down to the earth, and his angels were thrown down with him." John reiterates this in Revelation 20:2, "And he seized the dragon, that ancient serpent, who is the devil and Satan, and bound him for a thousand years."

Consider where our enemy is located in the Bible's overall story. First, God creates time and space. Second, He fills the space with water, plants, oxygen, and life-sustaining light. Third, He then creates living creatures and completes creation with mankind as His representative image-bearing steward.

Once God completes Creation, the enemy is introduced into the biblical narrative. This is an example of why all stories mirror the

Bible's stories. Stories have a protagonist—a hero—and an antagonist—a villain—whom the protagonist must overcome. The Bible's hero is Jesus because He saves mankind from death. The Bible's villain is Satan because he wants to destroy mankind. The struggle for mankind is why spiritual warfare exists. We know the hero wins the fight—and choose to be on His team or remain on the villain's team.

Back to Genesis 3:1, "Now the serpent was more crafty than any other beast of the field that the Lord God had made. He said to the woman, 'Did God actually say, "You shall not eat of any tree in the garden?"'" Like everything else in the creation story, the Lord God created the serpent. In other words, the story's villain was created by God. Since he was created, the enemy is bound by time like we are.

The first five words of the Bible, "In the beginning, God created," reveal that God existed before time began. Like us, the enemy is bound by time; thus, he cannot be equal to God.

In the creation stories, there are two types of living creatures: beasts and man.

Genesis 3:1 tells us the serpent is a created beast and does not bear the image of God; however, among the beasts, he is the most crafty. Other biblical versions use adjectives such as subtle, cunning, sneakier, clever, or shrewd instead of crafty. Crafty means to attain wants, desires, or ends using devious or deceitful means.

No other created beast was as cunning, deceitful, or scheming as the enemy; thus, the enemy's most remarkable attribute is that he will try to attain goals through deceit and subterfuge. The enemy is the least trustworthy of all beasts.

In John 8:44, Jesus reinforces this attribute when He tells a group of Pharisees, "You are of your father the devil, and your will is to do your father's desires. He was a murderer from the beginning and does not stand in the truth because there is no truth in him. When he lies, he speaks out of his own character, for he is a liar and the father of lies." According to Jesus, the enemy is more than crafty; he is "a murderer," "does not stand in the truth," "there is no truth in him," "he is a liar," and is "the father of lies."

The Lies Leading to Mankind's Fall

The second sentence of Genesis 3:1 begins with, "He said to the woman." At this point in the biblical story, the only two people in creation are the man and the woman.

The enemy talks to the woman because she is more susceptible to his guile, lies, and craftiness. She is more susceptible because she did not hear God's command directly. Genesis 2:16-17 states, "And the Lord God commanded the man, saying, 'You may surely eat of every tree of the garden, but of the tree of the knowledge of good and evil you shall not eat, for in the day that you eat of it you shall surely die.'" The woman could only know about God's command from the man.

Let's look at more of the conversation between the enemy and the woman in Genesis 3:1-5. "Now the serpent was more crafty than any other beast of the field that the Lord God had made. He said to the woman, 'Did God actually say, "You shall not eat of any tree in the garden"?' [2] And the woman said to the serpent, 'We may eat of the fruit of the trees in the garden, [3] but God said, "You shall not eat of the fruit of the tree that is in the midst of the garden, neither shall you touch it, lest you die.' [4] "But the serpent said to the woman, 'You will not surely die. [5] For God knows that when you eat of it your eyes will be opened, and you will be like God, knowing good and evil.""'

In the woman's rendition of God's command to the man, three differences exist.

The first difference occurs in Genesis 3:3, when she called the tree "in the midst of the garden" instead of what God named it in Genesis 2:17, "the tree of the knowledge of good and evil."

The second difference is that the woman added the phrase, "…neither shall you touch it," to God's command. Finally, when God spoke to the man, He ended His command by saying, "You shall surely die." The woman ended her quote of the command with, "lest you die."

These three misquotes by the woman might seem minor, but there is no such thing as "minor" mistakes when it comes to God's commands, particularly when a person is dealing with the enemy—whose primary characteristic is deceit.

Let's talk about the power of small things. In James 3, we see how small things, such as horse bits, ship rudders, and a person's tongue control larger things. In Luke 16, while talking to the Pharisees, Jesus stated that if a person is dishonest in little things, the dishonesty extends to larger things. In Matthew 25, Jesus gave the parable of the talents, representing how God gives more to those who are faithful with little. We need to interpret and use God's word carefully. Little mistakes can have dire consequences.

Let's see what happens following the woman's minor mistakes. Genesis 3:4-5 states, "But the serpent said to the woman, 'You will not surely die. For God knows that when you eat of it your eyes will be opened, and you will be like God, knowing good and evil.'"

God's original statement in Genesis 2:17 was, "You shall surely die." The serpent said, "You will not surely die" (Genesis 3:4). Our enemy, disguised as a serpent, slightly modified God's statement. Since the woman did not understand God's command as well as she should have, she went along with the serpent's minor addition. This example illustrates the enemy's primary tactic of blending his lies with a significant amount of truth.

In Genesis 3:5, the serpent appealed to the woman's pride by encouraging her to be like God when he stated, "For God knows that when you eat of it your eyes will be opened, and you will be like God, knowing good and evil." Mankind's natural heart is prone to fall to the temptation of pride. The enemy—who was kicked out of heaven because of pride—knows our weakness and uses it against us.

The fall of mankind occurs in Genesis 3:6: "So when the woman saw that the tree was good for food, and that it was a delight to the eyes, and that the tree was to be desired to make one wise, she took of its fruit and ate, and she also gave some to her husband who was with her, and he ate." The man and the woman, Adam and Eve, ate from the tree of the knowledge of good and evil, the one tree from which God told the man not to eat, or he would surely die. Let's examine why the woman ate the tree's fruit.

First, the woman saw that the tree was good for food. The woman convinced herself that the tree's fruit could provide nourishment. People have to eat. Pragmatically, eating the fruit made sense. The fact that the tree's fruit was good for food makes it better. Second, it was a delight to the eyes. The woman saw that the tree's fruit was beautiful. Not only was it useful as food, but it looked good. Third, the tree's fruit could make one wise. We are supposed to seek wisdom, right? Full of pride, the woman decided to take a shortcut to becoming wise. Because the woman did not fully understand God's command, she committed a sin that exemplifies the three sins common to all.

In 1 John 2:16, we see the woman's three sins in one sentence. "For all that is in the world—the desires of the flesh and the desires of the eyes and pride of life—is not from the Father but is from the world." Commonly stated, the three sins common to all people stem from the lust of the flesh, the lust of the eyes, and the pride of life.

The woman ate the fruit because "the tree was good for food [lust of the flesh], and that it was a delight to the eyes [lust of the eyes], and that the tree was to be desired to make one wise [pride of life]" (Genesis 3:6).

The Enemy's Tactics

The fall of mankind's story in Genesis 3:1-6 reveals the enemy's tactics.

1. First, attack the unprepared to establish a stronghold. The woman relied upon the man to be exact with God's command as a means of protection, as she did not hear God's command directly. She was susceptible to the enemy's attacks because she did not know God's exact commands.

2. Second, the enemy altered God's commands. He lied. Satan and his evil followers are highlighted and marked by lies. They will always lie. They are the enemies of the truth and will always try to undermine it.

3. Third, the enemy uses our desires to set traps for us. Our desires haven't changed since the first man and woman. We still want to satisfy our flesh's lustful desires for temporary pleasures. We want to possess what our eyes see. In our pride, we justify disobeying God's commands. Our enemy—the serpent, the devil, Satan—uses our desires, possessions, and pride to tempt us into choosing disobedience to God's will and commands.

Lesson Application - The application of Lesson 10 was to list what God has placed under your stewardship authority. Write down at least one item on the list that you know the enemy is trying to undermine using deceitful tactics. Then, write down what you, as the area's steward, can do to protect what God has placed under your authority.

Lesson 12

What Went Wrong

Context

The previous lesson focused on the enemy's role in the fall of mankind, found in Genesis 3:1-6. The lesson ended by highlighting the enemy's three tactics. The enemy establishes strongholds by attacking weaknesses. He always uses lies to undermine the truth and sets temptation traps that appeal to our desires, possessions, and pride.

This lesson examines the man's failures. Ecclesiastes 1:9 states, "What has been is what will be, / and what has been done is what will be done, / and there is nothing new under the sun." This verse lets us know the enemy is playing the same game today that he played with the first steward. He is playing the same game because we make the same mistakes Adam made. Understanding Adam's stewardship failures allows us to avoid making the same mistakes he made.

Adam's Mistakes

As stewards of our portion of God's creation, we need to understand the specific mistakes the first steward made so we don't repeat them in the future. His first mistake was that the woman did not know God's command word-for-word (Genesis 3:2). Adam did not properly teach

Eve the command he received from God, and this mistake influenced all the others in the fall of mankind.

Adam's second mistake was not interrupting Eve's discussion with the serpent to clearly restate God's command. It is possible that Adam was not present during the discussion between Eve and the serpent, but this is unlikely. Also, if the garden weren't fully secured—and remember, Adam was tasked with keeping the garden safe—why would Adam allow Eve to wander around by herself, especially since she did not know God's commands as well as she should have?

Third, why didn't Adam stop her once she decided to eat the fruit? Surely, he could have physically stopped her from eating the fruit and reiterated God's command so she could have made an informed decision. Again, whether Adam was co-located with Eve when she ate the fruit is debatable, but if he was not, his failure to properly teach her God's command while allowing her to roam around alone is even more pronounced.

Adam's final mistake was eating the very fruit God told him not to eat. Why would he partake of the fruit after seeing Eve disobey God's command? Only Adam and God can answer this question, but it appears Adam chose the woman's desires over God's commands.

Adam's failure as the steward of God's garden stems from his disobedience. Further, he failed to provide the leadership the woman needed. He failed to teach her exactly what God told him. He failed to intervene and assist her during the serpent's temptation. He failed to stop her from doing the one thing God told him not to do. Finally, he failed to put God's command above the woman's desires; he chose his wife over his Creator.

When confronted by God about their eating from the tree of the knowledge of good and evil, the man said in Genesis 3:12, "The woman whom you gave to be with me, she gave me fruit of the tree, and I ate." Not only did he fail to obey God and provide the woman with proper leadership, but he also failed to accept responsibility for his actions. The man God placed in charge of the garden blamed God for his failure.

God provided us with the story of Adam's failure so we can learn from his mistakes. Just as Adam, we have all failed to obey God's commands, but Jesus gives us the example of successful obedience. Let's look at how "the last Adam" successfully stewarded His disciples (1 Corinthians 15:45).

Jesus's Success

The Bible demonstrates that Jesus successfully stewarded His disciples to carry out the work He started. The first stewardship task of tending is covered in John 21:15-17, where Jesus asked Peter three times if Peter loved Him. After Peter's first affirmation of love, Jesus said, "Feed my lambs." After the second time, Jesus said, "Tend my sheep." After the third time, Jesus said, "Feed my sheep." Jesus stated the three messages to show Peter that he was forgiven for denying Jesus three times (John 18:15-18, 25-27). Jesus's nearly identical replies also reinforced Peter's mission of continuing the work Jesus started by feeding them the gospel of salvation. Romans 10:17 states, "So faith comes from hearing, and hearing through the word of Christ." Peter tended Jesus's flock by preaching the gospel to the early church.

On the second task of keeping, John 17:12-15 shows Jesus praying for His disciples to be protected after His earthly ministry ended. This portion of His prayer states, "While I was with them, I kept them in your name, which you have given me. I have guarded them, and not one of them has been lost except the son of destruction, that the Scripture might be fulfilled. [13] But now I am coming to you, and these things I speak in the world, that they may have my joy fulfilled in themselves. [14] I have given them your word, and the world has hated them because they are not of the world, just as I am not of the world. [15] I do not ask that you take them out of the world, but that you keep them from the evil one." Jesus testified that He protected the disciples and prayed that the Father would protect them after He physically left this world.

In the third task of exercising authority, we see that early in His ministry, Jesus renamed some of His chosen disciples. One such instance can be found in the opening chapter of John when Andrew brings his brother Simon to meet Jesus. Verse 42 reads, "Jesus looked at him and said, 'You are Simon the son of John; you shall be called Cephas' (which is translated Peter)." Jesus exercised His authority over Simon by giving him the name Peter.

Jesus commanded His disciples to exercise authority in renaming those they baptized. When He gave His Great Commission in Matthew 28:18-20, He stated, "All authority in heaven and on earth has been given to me. Go therefore and make disciples of all nations, baptizing them in the name of the Father and of the Son and of the Holy Spirit, teaching them to observe all that I have commanded you." The act of baptism is a public statement of a person's new identity as a child of the Father, a sibling of Jesus, and a vessel of the Holy Spirit.

In the fourth task of obedience, Jesus obeyed the Father's commands (John 5:19, 10:18, 12:49, and 14:10). While speaking to His disciples in John 14:15, Jesus stated, "If you love me, you will keep my commandments." Clearly, Jesus expected His disciples to be obedient. Notice how love for Jesus is the key to keeping His commandments. John, one of the disciples present when Jesus stated that obedience comes from love, later wrote in 1 John 4:19, "We love because he first loved us." When we fully recognize the love that our Lord Jesus Christ showed us, how can we not choose to love Him back?

Here are some of the highlights of Jesus's demonstration of love:

- God humbled himself to become human, Philippians 2:7;
- He did not retaliate against baseless persecution, Luke 23:13-24;

- ☐ He took on all of the world's sins, 1 Peter 2:24;
- ☐ He paid the penalty of death for our sins, 1 John 2:2; and,
- ☐ His sacrifice provided the opportunity for righteousness, 2 Corinthians 5:21.

Out of love for us, Jesus provided each of us the opportunity to be righteous before our Holy God. As discussed in Lesson 9, God's Spirit resides in the hearts of those who accept Jesus as their Lord and Savior, making them righteous. Righteousness is faith in God, demonstrated by obedience to His will.

Lesson Application - Obedience is the most important of the four tasks God has for all His stewards. Which of the other three tasks–tend, keep, and exercise authority–do you struggle with? Write the task with an explanation of why you need assistance. Use what you wrote down to ask God for specific assistance through prayer.

Lesson 13

Spiritual Warfare

Context

The previous lesson looked at the stewardship failures of the first Adam and the successes of the last Adam. The lesson ended with a discussion on how our obedience to God is inextricably tied to our decision to love Jesus.

In Matthew 10:16, Jesus told His disciples, "Behold, I am sending you out as sheep in the midst of wolves, so be wise as serpents and innocent as doves." He sent them to Jewish towns to train them for when His earthly ministry ended. In addition to preaching the Gospel, He empowered them to cast out demons and heal the sick. As they went out, Jesus told them to be wise and innocent because they would be like sheep among wolves.

The Three Wolves of Spiritual Warfare

This lesson explores the wolves Jesus wanted His disciples to be aware of when He could not physically maintain protection for them. There were three "wolves" of which the disciples needed to be wary. The first was demonic spirits under the leadership of Satan, the devil, the serpent, the dragon, Beelzebul, etc. Ephesians 6:12 states, "For we do not wrestle against flesh and blood, but against the rulers, against the authorities, against the cosmic powers over this present darkness, against the spiritual forces of evil in the heavenly places." Lesson 11 opened the discussion on the enemy.

The second wolf the disciples needed to be aware of was the world's system. The function of this world is based on a system dominated by Satan. It is anti-Jesus and seeks to undermine the desires of God. Jesus warned His disciples about this world while preparing them for His impending death. In John 15:18-19, He stated, "If the world hates you, know that it has hated me before it hated you. If you were of the world, the world would love you as its own; but because you are not of the world, but I chose you out of the world, therefore the world hates you." One of His disciples, John, affirmed what Jesus stated in 1 John 5:19, when he wrote, "…the whole world lies in the power of the evil one."

In his letter to the Church at Ephesus, Paul confirms that this world is ruled by the enemy. In Ephesians 2:1-3, he wrote, "And you were dead in the trespasses and sins in which you once walked, following the course of this world, following the prince of the power of the air, the spirit that is now at work in the sons of disobedience—among whom we all once lived in the passions of our flesh, carrying out the desires of the body and the mind, and were by nature children of wrath, like the rest of mankind." Because Satan is the ruler of this world, where most of the population is comprised of non-believers, the world's system is set against Jesus. Its politics, economics, education, entertainment, and religion lie in the power of the evil one, who is God's enemy.

The third wolf is ourselves. Our natural self, flesh, and heart desire self-gratification and will choose disobedience and sin. This is why God offers us His Spirit, which gives us a new heart to make choices that align with His will. Galatians 5:16-18 states, "But I say, walk by the Spirit, and you will not gratify the desires of the flesh. For the desires of the flesh are against the Spirit, and the desires of the Spirit are against the flesh, for these are opposed to each other, to keep you from doing the things you want to do. But if you are led by the Spirit, you are not under the law."

The wolves Jesus wanted His disciples to avoid during their training–demonic spirits, the world, and our fleshly desires–were present when we were born into this world. These three "wolves" are tied together, operating under the leadership of Satan and actively working against God's will. We are born into a world ruled by the enemy, who continuously tempts us to go against God's will.

Figure 2 - The Three Wolves

There Are Only Two Warring Factions

Have you ever heard the phrase, *We are all God's children*? The pain and suffering we see around us are blatant evidence that not all people are God's children. How is it that some are God's children and some are not? The answer is that the children of God are people who accept Jesus as Lord and Savior and receive God's Holy Spirit. John 1:12 states, "But to all who did receive him, who believed in his name, he gave the right to become children of God." Galatians 3:26 states, "For in Christ Jesus you are all sons of God, through faith." 1 John 5:1 states, "Everyone who believes that Jesus is the Christ has been born of God, and everyone who loves the Father loves whoever has been born of him."

Before accepting Jesus as Lord and Savior and becoming children of God, we are children of the devil because our fleshly bodies are born in a world system set up against Jesus and ruled by Satan. In John 8:44, Jesus condemned some religious leaders when He said, "You are of your father the devil, and your will is to do your father's desires. He was a murderer from the beginning, and does not stand in the truth, because there is no truth in him. When he lies, he speaks out of his own character, for he is a liar and the father of lies." 1 John 3:8-10 states, "Whoever makes a practice of sinning is of the devil, for the devil has been sinning from the beginning. The reason the Son of God appeared was to destroy the works of the devil. No one born of God makes a practice of sinning, for God's seed abides in him; and he cannot keep on sinning, because he has been born of God. By this it is evident who are the children of God, and who are the children of the devil: whoever does not practice righteousness is not of God, nor is the one who does not love his brother." The truth is, we are fleshly born children of the devil, but can become spiritual children of God.

This truth means that all people are either affiliated with the forces of Satan or with the forces of God. There is no neutral force. Anyone who believes they are abstaining from Satan's or God's force is fooling themselves. The abstainers belong to the world's system, which falls under Satan. In this world, we are born into a spiritual war that began long before we arrived—spiritual because God and angels, even the fallen ones like Satan, are spiritual. In John 4:24, Jesus states, "God is spirit, and those who worship him must worship in spirit and truth." Hebrews 1:14 states that angels are "ministering spirits." Matthew 25:41 states there is an "eternal fire prepared for the devil and his angels." Thus, our enemy and his demons are also spirits. For other verses that affirm God as spirit, see Colossians 1:15 and 1 Timothy 1:17.

Because the war is spiritual, we cannot see the warring forces. But we can see the effects. Examples at the organizational or national levels include despotic governments, the destruction of entire civilizations, and national, ethnic, racial, or religious genocide. At the family level, we see broken marriages, dysfunctional families, and suffering children. At the personal level, we see broken people who experience fatigue, anxiety, depression, stress, temptation, fear, despair, lies, and revenge.

According to the Bible—our one source of truth in this world—none of the effects of spiritual warfare is God's will. Jeremiah 29:11 states, "For I know the plans I have for you, declares the Lord, plans for welfare and not for evil, to give you a future and a hope." James 1:17 states, "Every good gift and every perfect gift is from above, coming down from the Father..." John 3:16 states, "For God so loved the world, that he gave his only Son, that whoever believes in him should not perish but have eternal life." Mark 10:18 tells us that only God is good.

Another way to think about the war into which we are born is that everything we do supports one of the two forces, whether we are consciously aware of our actions or not. If we are not operating within God's will, we are operating on behalf of God's enemy. Each decision you make, each thing you do, either supports God's desires for good or supports the evil desires of the lost who are children of the devil.

What Does God's Enemy Want?

The Bible tells us why Satan is evil and what he wants. He was a created angel who wanted to be worshipped and glorified like God. Two prophets, Isaiah and Ezekiel, quoted God with language biblical scholars believe is about Satan. Isaiah 14:13-14 states, "You said in your heart, 'I will ascend to heaven; above the stars of God I will set my throne on high; I will sit on the mount of assembly in the far reaches of the north; I will ascend above the heights of the clouds; I will make myself like the Most High.'" Ezekiel 28:12-17 contains a lengthy passage about Satan. Verses 12 and 13 state, "You were the signet of perfection, full of wisdom and perfect in beauty. You were in Eden, the garden of God;" And verse 17 states, "Your heart was proud because of your beauty; you corrupted your wisdom for the sake of your splendor." According to the Isaiah and Ezekiel passages, Satan's sin was pride, which originated in his heart. Once Satan, an angel created by God, decided he wanted to be like God, he was thrown out of heaven.

The same prophets, Isaiah and Ezekiel, write about the incident: Isaiah 14:12 states, "How you are fallen from heaven, O Day Star, son of Dawn! How you are cut down to the ground, you who laid the nations low!" Ezekiel 28:14-16 states, "You were an anointed guardian cherub. I placed you; you were on the holy mountain of God;...In the abundance of your trade you were filled with violence in your midst, and you sinned; so I cast you as a profane thing from the mountain of God, and I destroyed you, O guardian cherub, from the midst of the stones of fire."

The Apostle John described what appears to be the same event in Revelation 12:7-10: "Now war arose in heaven, Michael and his angels fighting against the dragon. And the dragon and his angels fought back, but he was defeated, and there was no longer any place for them in heaven. And the great dragon was thrown down, that ancient serpent, who is called the devil and Satan, the deceiver of the whole world—he was thrown down to the earth, and his angels were thrown down with him. And I heard a loud voice in heaven, saying, 'Now the salvation and the power and the kingdom of our God and the authority of his Christ have come, for the accuser of our brothers has been thrown down, who accuses them day and night before our God.'" Revelation 12:3-4 tells us one-third of the angels followed Satan's exit from heaven. Jesus affirms what happened when He told His disciples in Luke 10:18, "I saw Satan fall like lightning from heaven."

We don't know some details about the war, such as the exact timing, the hierarchy of angels, what it means to be a cherub, etc., but we do know that Satan was thrown out of heaven because of his narcissistic pride. He wanted to be like God and fought for the glory that belongs only to the Creator, not the created. Because we know this, we know how this affects us.

Those angels who were thrown out of heaven were the same evil spirits and demons Jesus cast out in the New Testament. For example, Mark 3:11 states, "And whenever the unclean spirits saw him, they fell down before him and cried out, 'You are the Son of God.'" Not only did they know who Jesus was, but they appeared to know their final outcome would be judgment and torment. Matthew 8:29 states, "And behold, they cried out, 'What have you to do with us, O Son of God? Have you come here to torment us before the time?'"

It appears those fallen angels know the timing of their final judgment, which Matthew 25 and Revelation 20 call the Great White Throne judgment. John 5:21-29 and 2 Corinthians 5:10 tell us that Jesus is the judge who will sit on the Great White Throne. As judge, He will divide the believers from the non-believers, according to Matthew 25:31-46. Revelation 20:10 and Matthew 25:41 tell us that non-believers, including the fallen angels, will spend eternity in torment, thrown into a lake of fire called hell.

Have you ever noticed how selfish losers *also* want everyone else to lose? Their mantra seems to be, "If I can't win, nobody wins." Satan and his fallen angels know they will eventually spend eternity in a place called hell, which is built specifically for them. Like selfish losers, their goal seems to be to get as many of God's image-bearers as possible to spend eternity in hell with them.

Satan's war is not with man; it is with God. He lost his battle to be worshipped like God, but according to 1 Peter 5:8, the war is ongoing because our "adversary the devil prowls around like a roaring lion, seeking someone to devour." As the pinnacle of creation and the bearers of God's image, mankind is the next best way to harm God and thwart His will. Destroying God's beloved image-bearers by blinding them to the salvation message of Jesus Christ or tearing down the testimony of believers are ways the eventual loser seeks to harm God.

Four Spiritual Warfare Facts

Let's close this lesson with four facts about the spiritual war into which we are born. The first spiritual warfare fact is that while Satan rules this world, he cannot do whatever he wants, particularly when it comes to righteous believers. God is sovereign, and His will supersedes everything else. Numerous passages in Scripture affirm God's sovereignty. Job 42:2 states, "I know that you can do all things, and that no purpose of yours can be thwarted." Psalms 115:3 and 135:6 both tell us that God "does all that he pleases." Proverbs 16:9 states, "The heart of man plans his way, but the Lord establishes his steps." 1 Timothy 6:15 tells us the Lord Jesus Christ "is the blessed and only Sovereign, the King of kings and Lord of lords." In Matthew 19:26, Jesus stated, "With God, all things are possible."

Further proof of God's sovereignty is that Satan has to get permission from God before attacking those protected by God. In the Book of Job, we see two passages where God tells Satan what he is allowed to do to Job. First, Job 1:12 states, "And the Lord said to Satan, 'Behold, all that he has is in your hand. Only against him do not stretch out your hand.' So Satan went out from the presence of the Lord." Job 2:6 states, "And the Lord said to Satan, 'Behold, he is in your hand; only spare his life.'" During the Last Supper scene in Luke 22, Jesus tells Peter, "Simon, Simon, Satan has asked to sift all of you as wheat. But I have prayed for you, Simon, that your faith may not fail. And when you have turned back, strengthen your brothers," verses 31-32.

Because of God's sovereignty, a second spiritual warfare fact is that believers of Jesus as Christ can commit sin but cannot be possessed by an evil spirit. We cannot be possessed because sovereign God lives in our hearts as the Holy Spirit (Ezekiel 36:26-27, Romans 5:5, and 1 Corinthians 6:19). In John 10, a Jewish crowd in Jerusalem asked Jesus if He was the Christ. In verses 27-30, Jesus responded, "My sheep hear my voice, and I know them, and they follow me. I give them eternal life, and they will never perish, and no one will snatch them out of my hand. My Father, who has given them to me, is greater than all, and no one is able to snatch them out of the Father's hand. I and the Father are one."

A third spiritual warfare fact is that the world into which our souls are physically born is temporary. This world's ruler knows his domain is temporary because of the Great White Throne judgment discussed earlier (Revelation 20 and Matthew 25). Other biblical passages confirm the temporary nature of this world. Malachi 4:1 states, "For behold, the day is coming, burning like an oven, when all the arrogant and all evildoers will be stubble. The day that is coming shall set them ablaze, says the Lord of hosts, so that it will leave them neither root nor branch." Second Peter 3:10-13 states, "But the day of the Lord will come like a thief, and then the heavens will pass away with a roar, and the heavenly bodies will be burned up and dissolved, and the earth and the works that are done on it will be exposed. Since all these things are thus to be dissolved, what sort of people ought you to be in lives of holiness and godliness, waiting for and hastening the coming of the day of God, because of which the heavens will be set on fire and dissolved, and the heavenly bodies will melt as they burn! But according to his promise we are waiting for new heavens and a new earth in which righteousness dwells." Because of the temporary nature of this world, Jesus tells His disciples in Matthew 10:28, "...do not fear those who kill the body but cannot kill the soul. Rather fear him who can destroy both soul and body in hell."

The fourth spiritual warfare fact the Bible tells us is that we are simply passing through this temporary world. First Chronicles 29:15 states, "For we are strangers before you and sojourners, as all our fathers were. Our days on the earth are like a shadow, and there is no abiding." Psalms 119:19 states, "I am a sojourner on the earth; / hide not your commandments from me!" Philippians 3:20 states, "But our citizenship is in heaven, and from it we await a Savior, the Lord Jesus Christ." Hebrews 11:13-16 states, "These all died in faith, not having received the things promised, but having seen them and greeted them from afar, and having acknowledged that they were strangers and exiles on the earth. For people who speak thus make it clear that they are seeking a homeland. If they had been thinking of that land from which they had gone out, they would have had opportunity to return. But as it is, they desire a better country, that is, a heavenly one. Therefore God is not ashamed to be called their God, for he has prepared for them a city." First Peter 2:11 states, "Beloved, I urge you as sojourners and exiles to abstain from the passions of the flesh, which wage war against your soul." This world is not our permanent residence; it is a place where we wait for God to call us home.

Men, our souls are physically born into a spiritual war caused by Satan, who wants as many of God's image-bearers as possible to end up in hell with him and his demons. But have faith because God is sovereign, and we are protected from evil spirit possession because His Spirit resides in our hearts. We will suffer in this world, but know that it is temporary and not our eternal home.

Lesson Application - Which of the four spiritual warfare facts gives you the most peace, solace, or *shalom* when considering the spiritual battles you face? Explain why.

Lesson 14

What God Expects

Context

The previous lesson discussed the basics of spiritual warfare, such as the composition of the two warring parties, the warfare's effects, and how image-bearers can choose on which side of the conflict they belong. This lesson reiterates spiritual warfare truths and outlines what God expects from us, men who have chosen to follow Jesus.

Spiritual Warfare Summation

A fundamental truth about the world's spiritual warfare begins with two opposing factions. One faction belongs to the enemy: Satan, the devil, fallen angels, etc. The other faction belongs to the Triune God and His heavenly angels. There are no other factions. No third option or neutral party exists.

As to people, everyone in this world is a member of one of those two factions. The one factor determining to which faction a person belongs is whether the person believes in Jesus as Lord and Savior or not. Biblical verses that substantiate this premise include John 1:12-13, Galatians 3:23-29, and 1 John 5:1-4. If the Bible is true, all who do not believe in Jesus are on the enemy's side, whether they are aware of their affiliation or not, and whether they believe in God, the devil, and spiritual warfare or not.

The next truth about spiritual warfare is that the war for supremacy in heaven has already been determined. The spiritual war that is occurring is taking place in this physical world that God created.

A summary of the spiritual warfare in this world is:

1. Satan and his followers have already lost the war for heaven (Is. 14:12-15, Ez. 28:12-17, Luke 10:18, & Rev. 12:7-9).
2. They know hell was built for them (Mt. 25:41).
3. They know Jesus will send them to hell (Mt. 8:29).
4. Some of the fallen angels are already chained in hell (2 Pet. 2:4).

We know from Satan's temptations of Eve and Jesus that he knows God's commands and His Word. In Genesis 3, Satan twisted God's command to trick Eve into eating from the tree of the knowledge of good and evil. When he tempted Jesus in Matthew 4:6, he quoted Psalm 91:11-12. Since he knows God's Word, he knows his final destination is hell, the everlasting fire prepared for him and his fallen angels, according to Matthew 25:41. When combined with Matthew 8:29, we see the fallen angels know there is a time when Jesus will place them in the everlasting fire as a form of torment, punishment, and torture.

The Enemy's Goal?

At this point, you may ask yourself why mankind is involved in the spiritual fight if the war for heaven is over and the enemy and his fallen angels know their final outcome? In response, let's start with Genesis 1:26-27, which tells us that only mankind, male and female, was made in God's image. The worst outcome for any image-bearer is to spend eternity away from their Creator whose image they bear in a place described as dark and filled with weeping and gnashing of teeth (Luke 13:28, Matthew 8:12, 22:13, and 25:30). While the Bible doesn't explicitly state this, Satan and the other fallen angels must want as many of God's image-bearers as possible to also end up in hell.

Dr. Billy Graham agreed with this hypothesis. In response to the question of whether the devil was real and if so, was Hell his home, the Reverend Graham responded that Satan "...knows what the end is for him. He made his choice long ago and wants to take a world of people with him to Hell. He does not want to serve out his eternal sentence alone." [3]

Numerous passages in Scripture, such as Romans 2:6-8, 2 Peter 2:1-11, and 1 John 3:8-10, tell us that unrepentant sin is how a person ends up in hell. Sin is mankind's problem. And sin is what the enemy encourages to get as many image-bearers to end up in hell with him. Faith in Jesus as Lord and Savior is a person's only method for being exonerated for their sin. Jesus is the only means of eternal salvation.

Because of this truth, Satan's strategy for bringing the souls of image-bearers to hell with him must be to prevent the gospel of salvation through faith in Jesus from being spread. He accomplishes his strategy on two fronts. The first front is with non-believers, whom the enemy encourages to love their sin. He has done such a good job on this front that John 15:18-19 tells us he dominates the entire world. A world filled with people who love their sin minimizes the opportunity for non-believers to hear the gospel of salvation.

On the believers' front, the enemy prevents people who have accepted the gospel message from spreading it to non-believers. He does this by trapping them in sin, causing anxiety and depression. Believers who are trapped in their own sin are less likely to tell others about the saving grace of Jesus and certainly lack a sincere conviction when they provide their testimony. As believers, we heard the gospel message before accepting Jesus as our Lord and Savior. As stewards of

---

[3] Graham, Billy. "Is there really a devil? And if so, is Hell his home?" Billy Graham Evangelistic Association. https://billygraham.org/answers/is-the-devil-real-if-so-is-hell-his-home

God's creation, we have an obligation to pass that message on to those whom God places in our circle of care.

What God Expects

We overcome the enemy's goal by starting with the knowledge that God's Spirit resides in the hearts of believers (1 Corinthians 6:19, Ezekiel 36:26-27, and Romans 5:5). Paul provides a lengthy discussion on what having God's Spirit means in Romans, Chapter 8. In verse five, he states, "Those who live according to the Spirit set their minds on the things of the Spirit."

God's Spirit lives in the hearts of all who have accepted Jesus as Lord and Savior. This is the same Spirit who created the world and all things in it—the timeless, eternal Spirit—the Spirit who offered us grace and eternal salvation. The Spirit reigns as the King of kings and Lord of lords—the Alpha and Omega.

All of us believers can set our minds to that Spirit. We can think what He thinks, become what He wants us to become. A good team is always more powerful than an individual. Imagine what could be accomplished when a team of believers simultaneously sets their minds on God's will. Building good teams is essentially the goal of the Discipled Warriors Ministry.

To understand what God expects from believers engaged in this world's spiritual war, let's remind ourselves of the commands our Lord and Savior, Jesus, stated were most important. In Matthew 22:37-40, a Pharisee lawyer tested Jesus by asking Him, "Teacher, which is the great commandment in the Law?"

Jesus responded with, "You shall love the Lord your God with all your heart and with all your soul and with all your mind. This is the great and first commandment. And a second is like it: You shall love your neighbor as yourself. On these two commandments depend all the Law and the Prophets." So, according to Jesus, loving God and loving our neighbors are the two most important commandments.

In John 14:15-17, Jesus told His disciples they would keep His commandments if they loved Him. According to Jesus, loving Him is the key to keeping His commandments—particularly those related to loving God and loving our neighbors. The Bible also tells us we should love Jesus because He first loved us (1 John 4:19). See Lesson 12 for some highlights of Jesus's demonstrated love for us. God expects believers who have become His children to obey Him. We demonstrate our obedience by loving Him and the other image-bearers with whom we exist.

Love is a Choice

Based on the previously mentioned biblical passages—Matthew 22:37-40, John 14:15-17, and 1 John 4:19—love has to be a choice. If the Lord commands us to love Him, love must be a choice. Because love is a choice, it cannot simply be a feeling or an emotion. When we recognize God's love for us, we can choose to love Him back and gain the ability to love others through obedience to God. We show our love for Him through obedience, striving to be righteous, and seeking to be without sin like Jesus was.

But we first have to recognize God's love for us. This is an act of thinking. The NKJV of Proverbs 23:7 states, "For as [a man] thinks in his heart, so is he." In other words, our knowledge and thoughts control who we are and who we will become. So, how do we know God loves us?

Again, we return to our only source of truth in this world, the Bible. John 3:16 states, "For God so loved the world, that he gave his only Son, that whoever believes in him should not perish but have eternal life." Romans 5:8 states, "But God shows his love for us in that while we were still sinners, Christ died for us." Jeremiah 31:3 states, "The Lord appeared to him from far away. I have loved you with an everlasting love; therefore I have continued my faithfulness to you." Psalm 86:15 states, "But you, O Lord, are a God merciful and gracious, slow to anger and abounding in steadfast love and faithfulness." Psalm 136:26 states, "Give thanks to the God of heaven, for his steadfast love endures forever." Deuteronomy 7:9 states, "Know therefore that the Lord your God is God, the faithful God who keeps covenant and steadfast love with those who love him and keep his commandments, to a thousand generations."

God's Love

As believers in Jesus who have His Holy Spirit residing in our hearts, God's love for us should be evident in our lives—*evident* because we should see the Holy Spirit at work in our lives. This is particularly in terms of the spiritual fruit listed in Galatians 5:22-23, which states, "But the fruit of the Spirit is love, joy, peace, patience, kindness, goodness, faithfulness, gentleness, self-control; against such things there is no law." If you have been a believer for a few years, you should know that you are more loving, joyful, peaceful, patient, kind, good, faithful, gentle, and self-controlled than you once were, which is proof that you are being transformed into who you were created to be.

God's Holy Spirit sanctifies us, transforming us into the likeness of His Son, Jesus. The longer we live in this world as believers who actively follow Jesus, the more spiritual fruit we should produce. Likeness does not mean the same. Likeness is similar to the fact that each book of the Bible is unique, yet each contains the same message of peace through the Messiah, Jesus.

The sanctification process doesn't mean we lose our identity. The process makes us more righteous, more like a sinless Jesus. A few Bible verses that substantiate the Spirit's sanctification include:

- Second Corinthians 3:18 states, "And we all, with unveiled face, beholding the glory of the Lord, are being transformed into the same image from one degree of glory to another. For this comes from the Lord who is the Spirit."

- First Corinthians 15:49 states, "Just as we have borne the image of the man of dust, we shall also bear the image of the man of heaven."

- First John 3:2 states, "Beloved, we are God's children now, and what we will be has not yet appeared; but we know that when he appears we shall be like him, because we shall see him as he is."

- There are numerous other verses, but to show the idea that transformation is not only a New Testament idea, but we also have Psalm 51:10-12, which says, "Create in me a clean heart, O God, and renew a right spirit within me. Cast me not away from your presence, and take not your Holy Spirit from me. Restore to me the joy of your salvation, and uphold me with a willing spirit."

Obedient Stewards

The transformation into the likeness of Jesus is God's method for equipping us to be obedient to Him while we exist and engage in a spiritual war. This makes sense when we consider the stewardship mission He has given to all men. Our ability to be obedient to God's will directly impacts our ability to be good stewards of His creation.

As a review, the four tasks of our stewardship mission are:

1. Tend, which is to make the living parts of creation healthy and fruitful.

2. Keep, which is to protect the living from internal and external threats.

3. Exercise authority, which is to lead and manage the portion of God's creation that He charged us with stewarding. And,

4. Obey, which is the only way we can properly tend, keep, and exercise authority in God's creation.

Because God is the only source of truth in this world, we can choose to obey Him and have success as His stewards, or we can choose to be obedient to something else and fail in our God-given stewardship mission. Choosing obedience to God is not just for some things. We have to choose obedience in all areas of our lives. Consciously allowing one or some sins in our lives is how the enemy insidiously occupies our hearts, causing us to make decisions that go against God and negatively impact our stewardship mission.

Strongholds

A discussion about strongholds appears in 2 Corinthians 10:3-6, which states, "For though we walk in the flesh, we are not waging war according to the flesh. [4] For the weapons of our warfare are not of the flesh but have divine power to destroy strongholds. [5] We destroy arguments and every lofty opinion raised against the knowledge of God, and take every thought captive to obey Christ, [6] being ready to punish every disobedience, when your obedience is complete." The strongholds discussed in verse four are defended positions of strength.

The walls of Jericho provide a physical biblical example. In Joshua 6, the people inside Jericho thought they could not be defeated because of their walls. God took down the walls by His power, not by the way a man would take down the walls. God had the Israelites walk around the city's walls for seven days, and then He made the walls fall.

In spiritual warfare, a stronghold is a place where the enemy has gained access to your heart, shaping your thoughts and actions. Spiritual strongholds are the sins that we won't let go of and are negatively influencing our ability to steward God's creation. It is the deal we made with the devil, thinking that he won't expand his evil if we give in, just a little bit, to our "lust of the flesh, lust of the eyes, and pride of life," as stated in 1 John 2:16. But he will expand his strongholds in an effort to place image-bearers in complete deprivation.

A stronghold is simply a launch point for further operations. When I was part of the Ranger Regiment, I led a stronghold-capturing team whose task was to parachute into an airfield and secure it so follow-on forces could fly in, land, and expand our force's footprint. We established the stronghold as the first step in expanding the war.

Verse four of 2 Corinthians 10 states, "the weapons of our warfare…have divine power to destroy strongholds." Those weapons are God's sovereign, divine power. In Matthew 19:26, Jesus stated, "With God all things are possible." God's power can remove the enemy's strongholds.

Verses five and six explain how the strongholds are removed. The weapons of God's divine power destroy enemy strongholds when we "take every thought captive to obey Christ," making our "obedience complete."

Summary and Review - Let's review the truths contained in this lesson.

1. Each of us begins our existence in this world as immortal souls with nonpermanent bodies.
2. We exist on the battleground of a spiritual war between God and Satanic forces.
3. Satan and his forces have lost heaven and currently exist in this world, but will ultimately end up in hell.
4. Their goal is to bring as many of us with them to hell as possible.
5. The spiritual war is over our immortal souls, which will end up with God in heaven or in hell with Satan and his fallen angels.
6. The moment we are born, our souls are destined for hell.

7. But God wants to save us from hell and gives us the opportunity to choose to have His Spirit live in our hearts, which translates to our souls existing with Him in heaven once our nonpermanent bodies die.

8. God offers us forgiving grace from our sins through faith in Jesus as the means for eternal salvation.

9. Souls who refuse Jesus are destined for hell.

10. The enemy does not want anyone to understand how eternal salvation works, so he and his forces encourage sin strongholds in the heart of every soul.

11. When we "take every thought captive to obey Christ," making our "obedience complete," God removes any strongholds the enemy has on us, allowing us to steward our portion of God's creation as He intended.

12. God wants us to become righteous stewards of His creation, spreading the Gospel message in word and deed.

Lesson Application - Recognizing God's love is the key to obedience to His will, which, in turn, destroys any strongholds the enemy may have on you. List as many examples as you can of how God has demonstrated His love for you.

Lesson 15

Removing Strongholds

Context

The previous lesson states that God expects obedience while we steward His creation and contend with this world's spiritual warfare. The lesson ended with a quote from 2 Corinthians 10:4-6 that God will destroy the enemy's strongholds in our hearts when we "take every thought captive to obey Christ," making our "obedience complete."

This lesson will explore how we take every thought captive to Christ, destroying strongholds and allowing us to be who God commands us to be: effective stewards of His creation. Effectiveness requires us to eliminate the things that encourage sin and to be healed from its effects.

Sanctification Requires Prayer

Jesus is the way we get cleaned and healed from sin. Remember He is the LORD God—He is Yahweh. His power is unlimited; there is nothing He can't do, no place He can't go. He made Himself known so we could be saved from sin's death sentence.

I once heard someone say, "Jesus is not a rapist." That stuck with me. Jesus does not force Himself on anyone. We must ask Him into our hearts. We choose our eternal salvation; it is not forced upon us. Jesus not only wants us to be saved from sin's penalty of death, but also to live free from sin.

Sanctification is the process of learning to be free from sin and healed from the damage of past sin. In the sanctification process, God transforms us into the likeness of Jesus, who is holy and pure. Sanctification requires a deepening relationship with God, marked by regular conversations with Him. These conversations are prayers.

Jesus prayed a lot. When you read the Gospels, you cannot help but see that our Lord and Savior prayed often. Examples include Matthew 14:23, "And after he had dismissed the crowds, he went up on the mountain by himself to pray." Mark 1:35, "And rising very early in the morning, while it was still dark, he departed and went out to a desolate place, and there he prayed." Luke 6:12, "In these days he went out to the mountain to pray, and all night he continued in prayer to God." John 6:1, "Jesus then took the loaves, and when he had given thanks, he distributed them to those who were seated." Here's a question that provides insight: If Jesus is God, why did He pray?

The answer is that the Son was praying to the Father. In chapters five, six, and seven of John, Jesus informs His audience that He did not leave heaven to do His will but the will of the Father. In John 5:36, Jesus states, "For the works that the Father has given me to accomplish, the very works that I am doing, bear witness about me that the Father has sent me." In John 6:38, He states, "For I have come down from heaven, not to do my own will but the will of him who sent me." John 7:16-18 states, "So Jesus answered them, 'My teaching is not mine, but his who sent me. If anyone's will is to do God's will, he will know whether the teaching is from God or whether I am speaking on my own authority. The one who speaks on his own authority seeks his own glory; but the one who seeks the glory of him who sent him is true, and in him there is no falsehood.'"

Jesus talked to and received instructions from the Father. In John 12:49, Jesus states, "For I have not spoken on my own authority, but the Father who sent me has himself given me a commandment—what to say and what to speak." In Mark 10:45, Jesus states, "For even the Son of Man came not to be served but to serve, and to give his life as a ransom for many."

Like us, who steward a portion of God's creation, Jesus was in this world to serve God's will. We fully serve God's will when we are cleansed and free of sin. Second Timothy 2:21 states, "Therefore, if anyone cleanses himself from what is dishonorable, he will be a vessel for honorable use, set apart as holy, useful to the master of the house, ready for every good work."

Confessional Prayer

Jesus's early ministry lets us know our enemy's goals. In Luke 4:43, Jesus stated that His purpose was to preach the good news about God's kingdom. If preaching the good news about God's kingdom was Jesus's purpose, the enemy's goal is not to have the good news preached.

We have all been attacked by our common enemy. None of God's image-bearers is immune. The enemy's goal for non-believers is to prevent them from ever hearing the Gospel, keeping them trapped in their sinful state. The enemy's goal for believers is to prevent them from sharing the good news about God's kingdom with non-believers. Sin is how he accomplishes both goals.

The enemy has been around since creation. He knows our human tendencies to satisfy lustful desires, take possession of God's creation, and our pride. He knows how to use temptations to get us to sin willfully. Sin causes people to experience fear, frustration, loss, and a sense of failure. Sin is part of our human experience. We can limit sin, but until we die or Jesus returns, our decomposing bodies of flesh are predisposed to sin. Sin makes believers feel unworthy of sharing the

Gospel message, thus preventing us from effectively stewarding what God has placed in our sphere of influence.

While we cannot remove all sin from our lives, 1 Corinthians 1:30 tells us that our righteousness and sanctification are assured through Jesus. Thus, we believers must remember that our sin does not separate us from God. First John 1:8-10 tells us that when we sin, we must confess it before the Lord, knowing He forgives us.

Prayer is how we confess. Our confessional prayer should be detailed and honest, so we actively understand our proclivity to specific sins. Understanding how the enemy attacks us and establishes strongholds of sin in our hearts is crucial for preventing similar future attacks.

Practicing The 5Ws and H Method

A successful attack from the enemy establishes a stronghold or expands sin from an already established stronghold. The attack could have been in the past. It could be happening now. It could have happened numerous times. The point is to understand how the enemy's attack was successful so we can ask Jesus for specific assistance through prayer.

A method used by the military to collect specific details is called *the 5Ws and H*, which stand for Who, What, When, Where, Why, and How. I used this method hundreds of times for a variety of operations, and the method works for understanding how the enemy establishes or expands strongholds.

A blank 5Ws and H method of describing a stronghold-establishing attack is listed below, along with a summary for each. Think of a recent or memorable attack that established a sin stronghold in your life. Then, spend ten minutes writing as many facts about that attack as possible.

Who - *who was attacked?* Just you or someone you are responsible for?

What - *what happened?* What was the attack's effect? What damage was caused? Who or what was harmed?

When - *when was the attack?* Years ago? Recently? Currently? Be specific. Is the attack recurring?

Where - *where was the attack in relation to your spheres of influence?* Did this happen in your home and affect your family? Does it affect your coworkers at work? In your community? Elsewhere?

Why - *why was the enemy given access?* If God made you the steward over an area, why did you let your guard down to let the enemy in? Does 1 John 2:16's "lust of flesh," "lust of the eyes," or "pride of life" describe why the attack was successful? Was his stronghold established because of your ignorance/love of sin? Ultimately, what was the enemy's access point in establishing a stronghold?

How - *how could you have prevented the established stronghold?* As stewards, we are responsible for keeping our God-given areas safe. What could you or should you have done to prevent or deny the enemy's successful attack?

Lesson Application – Prayer Exercise

Now that you have listed details about the establishment of one sin stronghold in an area for which you are responsible, you can ask Jesus for His specific assistance in removing the stronghold and/or healing the stronghold's damage. Psalm 103:3 tells us the Lord "forgives all your sins" and "heals all your diseases." Jesus stated in Matthew 11:28-30, "Come to me, all who labor and are heavy laden, and I will give you rest. Take my yoke upon you, and learn from me, for I am gentle and lowly in heart, and you will find rest for your souls. For my yoke is easy, and my burden is light." Whatever baggage you are carrying, give it to our Savior. He wants us to live a life of freedom, not a life in chains (Luke 4:18).

Find a quiet place to conduct the stronghold-removing prayer exercise. In Matthew 6:16, Jesus told His disciples, "When you pray, go into your room and shut the door and pray to your Father who is in secret. And your Father who sees in secret will reward you." Remove all potential distractions such as cell phones, TVs, etc. Then, establish spiritual authority over the place by saying out loud, "In the name, power, and authority of Jesus, I command all spirits to be silent except for the Father, Son, and Holy Spirit."

Now you are ready to speak with God. His Spirit lives in us, so we don't need to pray out loud to Him, but you can if you feel led to do so. First, admit your stewardship failure to what the Father has placed in your hands. Use what you wrote down for the attack's five Ws and H to be specific in the details of your failure.

Then, ask Jesus to remove any remnants of the enemy's stronghold that may remain in your heart. Remember, Jesus is God. He can heal you by casting out any demonic strongholds you may have. Because He is not bound by time, He can heal strongholds established years ago. Then, ask the Spirit for the tools, strength, and wisdom to deny the enemy the same stronghold in the future.

Perform this same exercise with other strongholds the enemy may have over you. You may need to perform the exercise multiple times for long-lasting strongholds or debilitating wounds. As you conduct the other *five Ws and H* prayer exercises, give yourself time to adjust to God's renovation of your heart so you can see His Spirit working on you. Seeing Him at work will mature and deepen your faith.

Write down highlights of your prayer-exercise experience.

Lesson 16

Comm Lines

Context

The last lesson, Removing Strongholds, highlighted the power of prayer in our pursuit of becoming the men God created us to be. The lesson concluded with a prayer exercise to ask Jesus to remove our strongholds of sin. This lesson is titled "Comm Lines," a shortened term for "Lines of Communication," a term borrowed from military operations. Prayer is one of the four Comm Lines we Kingdom Warriors must use to have victory during spiritual warfare.

Comm Lines

In the military, the term "Comm Lines" is used by warfighting units to discuss the importance of communicating with higher, lower, and adjacent units. In combat, maintaining Comm Lines allows personnel and units to deconflict battle space responsibilities and avoid friendly fire incidents. Comm Lines also represent physical structures used to resupply needed gear, ammunition, food, and fuel. Those physical Comm Lines include airfields, roads, shipping channels, railroads, the internet, and satellites.

Established Comm Lines are used to receive external assistance from other kinetic units such as planes, helicopters, artillery, and air defense. Established Comm Lines allow external assistance from non-kinetic units, such as Psyops, Civil Affairs, Chaplains, and Medevac points, to evacuate the wounded from the battlefield. Battlefield Comm Lines are of the utmost importance because no one wins alone. Establishing and maintaining Comm Lines is the difference between winning and losing, life and death.

Men, we are born into a spiritual war over the eternal home of God's image bearers. In war, whether we like it or not, we are on one of two teams—the enemy's team or God's team. There is no third option. To make the situation more dire, the enemy rules this world, meaning the world's system is governed by the spirit that wants to "kill, steal, and destroy," according to John 10:10.

The military knows Comm Lines are vital to the success of physical warfare. How much more important are they to the spiritual battles we fight every day? That's a redundant question, but let me ask a few more to clarify and bolster the point.

Who created everything we see, touch, hear, taste, and smell? Who put us here and gave us the purpose, task, and mission of stewarding a portion of creation? Who loved us enough to pay for our sins? Shouldn't we be in constant communication with Him? Shouldn't we establish and maintain effective Comm Lines with our Creator, who sacrificed Himself out of love for us?

During His Sermon on the Mount, in Matt 7:11, Jesus stated, "If you then, who are evil, know how to give good gifts to your children, how much more will your Father who is in heaven give good things to those who ask him!" Thankfully, believers have a spiritual Father who loves us and provides us with four Comm Lines to use in our spiritual fights.

Comm Line 1 - He Made Himself Known

The first Comm Line is that He made Himself known to us. Ecclesiastes 3:11 tells us God "put eternity into our hearts." Romans 1:19-20 tells us He made Himself known to the world; no one can honestly say they don't know God exists. The Bible confirms that God wants all people to know He is present in their lives. Miraculously, God makes Himself known to the entire world while simultaneously maintaining a distinct, unique relationship with each person.

Your unique story of how you came to know God and accept Jesus is part of your testimony. If you have not already done so, take the time to write your story. Use it as a reminder of whose team you are on and how our Creator reached out to you.

Additionally, become attuned to seeing God and His handiwork in the world. At the very least, we should see this in the other creatures around us. In Genesis 6:17, 7:15, and 7:22, the Bible tells us that all air-breathing creatures have the breath of life. The original Hebrew word for the breath of life is "ruah," the same word used for God's Spirit in Genesis 1:2. Thus, the lungs of all air-breathing creatures are filled with God. Life is precious because it is produced and sustained by God. We should see Him in the living things around us, as well as in the wonders of nature.

Comm Line 2 - The Bible

The second Comm Line is the Bible, the collected sixty-six books authored by God's Holy Spirit through the writings of at least forty diverse men over 1,500 years. The story that connects those sixty-six books is the creation, fall, and redemption of mankind. A brief explanation of that story begins with the Bible providing a creation story that everyone understands, even if they choose not to accept the story.

The Bible also provides the standards expected of everyone to remain in a proper relationship with this world's Creator and eventually get to heaven. All people—even non-believers—understand there is a place called heaven. Further, all people understand that failure to meet certain standards means they will not go to heaven. A common term for those standards is the Law. Biblical stories display the inability of people to meet the Law's standards.

But the one who created this world intervened, so we don't have to meet the Law's standards to get to heaven. God in human form not only met the standards, but He accepted the penalty for our failures to meet those same standards. Jesus's sacrificial act allows for our redemption; we do not have to pay the price of eternal separation from God because of our sins. The Bible's main storyline focuses on God's redemptive act, so every person's soul has the opportunity to go to heaven when their bodies die.

The Bible also contains the policies, procedures, and practices common to all people on how to live in this world. It is an SOP, the acronym for Standing Operating Procedures. Many organizations use SOPs to establish common practices for all personnel, which assists in smooth, efficient operations. The Bible is our SOP for how to live in this temporary world, which is a spiritual battlefield. If we are true believers in and followers of Jesus, we must take the time to know and understand God's SOP to learn how to live. Don't think you have to understand the Living Word fully. God will use your disciplined, routine reading and studying to shape you into the man He wants you to be.

In John 5:39, Jesus told Jews who hated Him and were seeking to kill Him, "You search the Scriptures because you think that in them you have eternal life; and it is they that bear witness about me." Like all people, the Hebrew audience Jesus spoke to were seeking eternal life. They wanted to end up in heaven. Unlike most people, they understood God's Word was important to securing eternal life;

however, while they searched the Scriptures for the keys to eternal life, they failed to understand Jesus was the redeemer they needed. The Jews who did not recognize Jesus as the Messiah-Redeemer did not have the Holy Spirit. We need God's Spirit to understand God's Word fully. In John 14:25-26, Jesus told His disciples, "These things I have spoken to you while I am still with you. But the Helper, the Holy Spirit, whom the Father will send in my name, he will teach you all things and bring to your remembrance all that I have said to you."

In 1 Corinthians 2:10-14, we are told the Holy Spirit is required to interpret Scripture:

> "These things God has revealed to us through the Spirit. For the Spirit searches everything, even the depths of God. For who knows a person's thoughts except the spirit of that person, which is in him? So also no one comprehends the thoughts of God except the Spirit of God. Now we have received not the spirit of the world, but the Spirit who is from God, that we might understand the things freely given us by God. And we impart this in words not taught by human wisdom but taught by the Spirit, interpreting spiritual truths to those who are spiritual. The natural person does not accept the things of the Spirit of God, for they are folly to him, and he is not able to understand them because they are spiritually discerned."

Comm Line 3 - The Holy Spirit

God's Holy Spirit is our third Line of Communication. Merriam-Webster defines holy as "exalted or worthy of complete devotion as one perfect in goodness and righteousness." Because God is without sin, He is the only one worthy of our worship. Let's remind ourselves of some Scripture about the Holy Spirit.

Genesis 1:2 states, "The earth was without form and void, and darkness was over the face of the deep. And the Spirit of God was hovering over the face of the waters." Ezekiel 36:27 states, "I will put

My Spirit within you and cause you to walk in My statutes, and you will be careful to observe My ordinances." Romans 8:11 states, "But if the Spirit of Him who raised Jesus from the dead dwells in you, He who raised Christ Jesus from the dead will also give life to your mortal bodies through His Spirit who dwells in you." 1 Corinthians 3:16 states, "Do you not know that you are a temple of God and that the Spirit of God dwells in you?"

Second Timothy 1:14 reiterates, "The Holy Spirit…dwells within us." Think about that for a moment. Sinless, holy God resides in the hearts of believers. If we choose to listen to Him, He will direct us to live as righteous warriors amidst this world's spiritual warfare.

First Kings 19:12 tells us the Holy Spirit is the "still, small voice" that speaks to us if we listen to Him. John 17:14-15 tells us that when we listen to the Holy Spirit's directions, we can be in the world but not of the world. According to Ephesians 6:18, Colossians 4:2, and 1 Thessalonians 5:17, that still, small voice is how we can always be in prayer.

Comm Line 4 - Prayer

Prayer is the fourth Comm Line. There are at least five reasons why we should be in constant prayer. First, prayer is how we seek God's favor. In Exodus 32, Moses prayed for God's mercy on the nation of Israel after they had made a golden calf to worship. Verse fourteen tells us that after Moses's prayer for God's favor, "the LORD relented from the disaster that he had spoken of bringing on his people."

Second, prayer is how we pour out our souls to the LORD. First Samuel 1 tells the story of Hannah, the barren wife of Elkanah, who went to the temple to pray. While she silently prayed, tears rolled down her face, which Eli, the temple priest, mistook for a drunken woman's confession of sin. He confronted her, and in verse fifteen, Hannah replied, "No, my lord, I am a woman troubled in spirit. I have drunk neither wine nor strong drink, but I have been pouring out my soul before the LORD." Eli then blessed her, and soon afterward, Hannah conceived and gave birth to the prophet Samuel.

The third reason we pray is to cry out to heaven. Second Chronicles 32 contains the story of the Assyrian army surrounding Jerusalem. The situation is dire for the city, but verse twenty tells us, "Then Hezekiah the king and Isaiah the prophet, the son of Amoz, prayed because of this and cried to heaven." After the men cried out to heaven in prayer, the LORD saved Jerusalem from destruction by sending an angel who, according to Isaiah 37:36, slew 185,000 Assyrians, keeping Jerusalem safe.

The fourth reason we pray is to draw near to God. Psalm 73 opens with a lengthy discussion about how evildoers appear to prosper in this world. The Psalmist then tells of how the wicked will eventually fall to ruin, and then ends with verse twenty-eight, which states, "But for me it is good to be near God / I have made the LORD God my refuge / that I may tell of all your works." The point of Psalm 73 is that, regardless of what the world displays as success, we must stay close to the Sovereign God to avoid certain ruin.

The fifth reason for prayer is that it forces us to kneel before Almighty God. Paul opens Ephesians 3 with a discussion of the blessings God has provided him so that he could preach the Gospel to the Gentiles. He suffered for preaching, but wanted his readers to know he was not worried about his circumstances. In verse fourteen, he wrote, "For this reason, I bow my knees before the Father." Paul bows to God and submits his personal well-being to the LORD's will.

Comm Lines Summarized

God offers us four Lines of Communication that tell us how to live and operate within this spiritual battlefield. First, we know He exists, and nature reflects His handiwork. Second, the Bible explains His will. It provides specific guidance on operating in this world and the wisdom needed for our discernment of good and evil. Third, His Spirit resides in the hearts of Jesus-believers and guides them in all activities. Finally, God hears the prayers of the righteous. Prayer allows us to communicate directly with our Creator.

Even though He was God in the flesh, Jesus prayed often to receive specific commands from the Father. As the stewards of God's Creation, shouldn't we seek to hear from God just as our Lord and Savior did? Our next lesson will build on this lesson by discussing how to set the conditions for hearing directly from God.

Lesson Application - Which of the four Comm Lines allows you to understand God's will best? Provide one example of how you have experienced God's directions in this Comm Line.

Lesson 17

Hearing from God

Context

The last lesson covered our four Lines of Communication with God, our true commander-in-chief. Because "God is Spirit," using Comm Lines is necessary to survive and thrive in this world's spiritual warfare (John 4:24). The first Comm Line is that He has made His existence known to everyone, and the natural world confirms His continuing handiwork. The second, third, and fourth Comm Lines are given to the righteous or those who believe in Jesus as Lord and Savior.

Our second Comm Line is the Bible. According to 1 Corinthians 2:14, it can only be fully understood using the power of the Holy Spirit. God's Spirit residing in our hearts is the third Comm Line we have with our commander (Romans 5:5). He is with us at all times, illuminating biblical truths, giving us spiritual gifts, and providing us with wisdom and guidance. The fourth Comm Line we have with God is prayer, which is offered to the righteous (1 Pet 3:12). We can always talk to our Creator.

Prayer is a Choice

In the chaos of battle, always remember that we have been tasked with stewarding a portion of God's creation. We serve Him, not ourselves. We are not here for our benefit; we are here for His glory and His Kingdom. Being in the right alignment with God helps us maintain our obedience to Him, which enables us to tend, keep, and maintain authority over the portion of creation we are assigned. According to Jeremiah 29:13 and Matthew 6:33, obediently seeking God's will is a choice.

When we choose not to pray, listen to the Holy Spirit, study Scripture, or recognize God's sovereignty, we're saying that we are smart enough and good enough to steward the portion of God's creation we are responsible for without His guidance. Sometimes, we know we need God's guidance, but don't know exactly what to ask for. Thankfully, Romans 8:26 tells us the Holy Spirit speaks for us when we don't know what to say.

Jesus often used the fourth Comm Line of prayer to receive the Father's guidance. We've covered that the Bible exhibits multiple types of prayer—seeking God's favor, pouring out one's soul, crying out to heaven, drawing near, and kneeling before God. A routine prayer life ensures we stay humble before God. Second Chronicles 7:14, Psalms 25:9, Proverbs 11:2, Philippians 2:3, and James 4:6 & 10 all confirm this. Prayer helps us avoid the "Pride of Life" sin, which is the same sin that caused the fall of Satan and mankind. Prayer aligns us with God's will, and receiving His guidance and wisdom is key to victory over our spiritual battles.

Truths About Prayer

Most people have not had a conversation with God—actual words, admittedly in your mind, that you know are spoken by our Lord. God has often talked to me through the Spirit's "still small voice." I know it is Him, but His words are not distinct or memorable. I could not tell you exactly what He said, but I know His intent. I've had a few experiences in which I distinctly remember His words, and those have been unforgettable for me. I consider those distinct experiences as God speaking to me; one was definitely with Jesus, and the other was definitely with the Father. Both times I clearly heard from God had similar conditions that this lesson will share.

Before we cover how to set the conditions to hear from God, we need to revisit some truths about prayer. We who are created beings not only can talk directly to our Creator but are encouraged and commanded to have a continuous, personal relationship with the one whom we wholly depend on for life. Proverbs 15:29 and John 9:31 tell us God hears the prayers of the righteous. A simple definition of prayer is a communication between God and the righteous. Romans 1:17 and 2 Corinthians 5:21 tell us righteous people are those who believe in Jesus as Lord and Savior. We believers can be confident that God hears our prayers.

Prayer is a gift that unbelievers do not have. It is a privilege given to us out of God's love for us. We are foolish when we do not employ it in our lives. Further, God wants a continuous, personal relationship with us.

Revelation 3:20 states, "Behold, I stand at the door and knock. If anyone hears my voice and opens the door, I will come in to him and eat with him, and he with me." Hebrews 11:6 lets us know we have to want the relationship. "And without faith it is impossible to please him, for whoever would draw near to God must believe that he exists and that he rewards those who seek him." Matthew 11:28-29 promises our seeking Him is worth it. "Come to me, all who labor and are heavy laden, and I will give you rest. Take my yoke upon you, and learn from me, for I am gentle and lowly in heart, and you will find rest for your souls."

Hearing from God starts with the right attitude of wanting to hear from Him. In John 10:27, Jesus stated, "My sheep hear my voice, and I know them, and they follow me." Seek Him with a pure heart. In Matthew 5:8, Jesus stated, "Blessed are the pure in heart, for they shall see God." Once we get our attitude right, a few actions can help set the right conditions.

Before continuing to this lesson's application, review your notes from Lesson 3.

Lesson Application - Instructions for Hearing from God

The application for this lesson is similar to the Prayer Exercise from Lesson 15.

- Find a quiet place where you won't be disturbed or distracted. Matthew 6:6 states, "But when you pray, go into your room and shut the door and pray to your Father who is in secret. And your Father who sees in secret will reward you."

- Establish temporary authority over the place by saying out loud, "In the name, power, and authority of Jesus, I command all voices to be silent except for the Father, the Son, and the Holy Spirit." We speak out loud because only God can read our minds. Other spirits that may occupy the room, particularly demonic spirits, cannot read our minds.

- Take your time in getting your attitude right. This is the most critical step. Do not allow anything else to distract you while you focus on talking to God.

- Start by telling God you want to hear from Him. Admit your sins and ask for forgiveness so He will purify your heart. Tell God about your faith in Him and how you know Him.

- Tell Jesus how you know He is your Lord and Savior.

- Open your heart to hear from your Lord and Savior. Know that He finds you worthy of His sacrifice. Tell Him you know He died for your sins out of His love for you and obedience to His Father.

- Once your heart is clean and your attitude is right, ask Jesus a simple question to which you already know the answer. The simplest question you could ask is, "Jesus, do you love me?"

- Listen for His response. Perhaps it will be words, perhaps an emotion, perhaps something else. Be ready to receive and patiently wait for Jesus to respond to your question.

If you don't receive a response after a period of time that only you and the Holy Spirit can determine, reset the conditions and try again. A summary of those conditions begins with finding a quiet place and establishing authority over the space. Purifying your heart before the Lord your God and asking Him a question to which you already know the answer.

Always be mindful that we serve Jesus, not the other way around, but He does want us to have His assurance of eternal life. And He wants us to know we are members of God's family. Ultimately, He wants us to take up our cross and follow Him. When in doubt, ask God's Spirit to lead you and confirm what you already know so your faith in our Lord and Savior deepens.

Use the space below to write down specific details about your Hearing from God exercise, such as the time, place, and how God spoke to you. You may find a future review of your experience encouraging.

Details of the Hearing from God exercise

Lesson 18

Good and Bad Stewards

Context

Our previous lesson explained how to establish temporary authority over the space you occupy, setting the conditions for improving your ability to hear from God. Stewards effectively manage their portion of creation by routinely hearing from God and following His will. Our example, Jesus, demonstrated the routine practice of prayer with the Father.

This lesson will explore the characteristics of ineffective stewardship. The root cause of poor stewardship is a lack of obedience to God's will.

Our Flesh Is Disobedient

The problem with obedience to God is that His (and our) enemy, Satan, actively tempts us to sin. He wants us to be disobedient to God—just as he and his followers are. As a reminder, Satan's plan to hurt God is to bring as many image-bearers with him to hell as possible, and our unrepentant sin is how we end up there. Thankfully, Jesus not only offers us the opportunity to have our sins forgiven but also for our spiritual hearts to receive the Holy Spirit. God's Holy Spirit strengthens our hearts through sanctification, converting them over time to be more in line with Jesus.

However, the natural physical flesh within which our spiritual hearts exist opposes the Holy Spirit's sanctification. In Matthew 26:41 and Mark 14:38, Jesus told Peter, James, and John to be alert and pray because "…the spirit is willing, but the flesh is weak." Like the disciples in the Garden of Gethsemane, we may want to be obedient, but our natural flesh is easily tempted to sin.

In Romans 7:14-20, the Apostle Paul wrote how his flesh continually desires sin even though his renewed mind and heart only want righteousness. Additionally, right before he explained the Fruit of the Spirit in Galatians 5, Paul stated our bodies are opposed to God's Spirit in verses sixteen and seventeen, which state, "But I say, walk by the Spirit, and you will not gratify the desires of the flesh. For the desires of the flesh are against the Spirit, and the desires of the Spirit are against the flesh, for these are opposed to each other, to keep you from doing the things you want to do."

In summation, our natural bodies will oppose our spiritual desire to be good stewards of God's creation. This condition will not change until we are given resurrected, glorified bodies at Jesus's return. When Paul compared our earthly bodies to tents in 2 Corinthians 5:1-9, he implicitly argued that our souls will one day live in a non-transitory structure, a permanent home. He explicitly wrote about where our souls will reside in Philippians 3:20-21, which stated, "...we await a Savior, the Lord Jesus Christ, who will transform our lowly body to be like his glorious body, by the power that enables him even to subject all things to himself."

The Apostle John agreed with Paul when he wrote in 1 John 3:2, "Beloved, we are God's children now, and what we will be has not yet appeared; but we know that when he appears we shall be like him…" Paul and John both wrote that—like the resurrected Jesus—we will have perfect, immortal bodies in our resurrection. When that happens, our bodily flesh will no longer be in opposition to God's Spirit as it is now.

Obedient Stewardship

God gave this world's first steward, Adam, the directions for maintaining the peaceful existence in which he was placed. Genesis 2:15-23 lists the four stewardship tasks necessary to maintain shalom with God. As a reminder, God's four tasks to stewards are to tend, keep, and exercise authority while maintaining obedience. The graphic below shows how the four stewardship tasks work in unison.

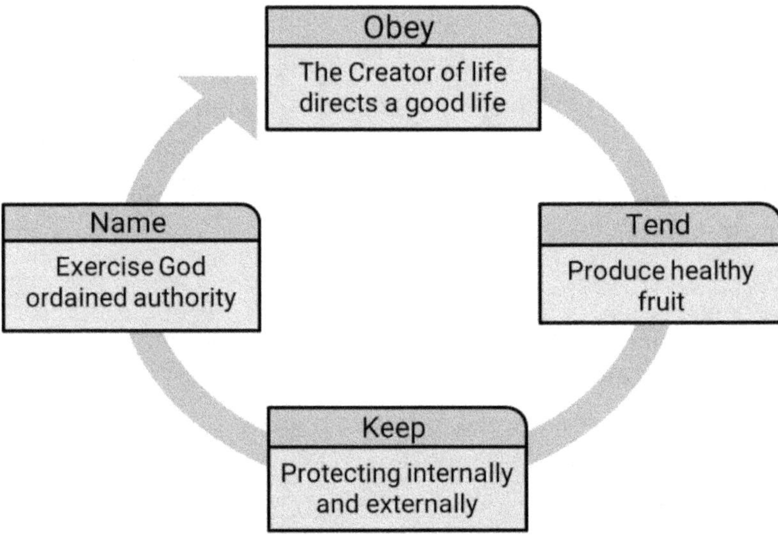

Figure 3 - Obedient Stewardship Cycle

Effectively tending a portion of God's creation can occur once the steward chooses to obey God. Synonyms for *tending* include working, cultivating, watering, feeding, planting, shearing, maintaining, managing, nurturing, nursing, ministering, etc. One of God's miracles is for living things to produce healthy fruit. Tending is providing what the living thing needs to be healthy and fruitful.

God also tells His stewards to keep the portion of the creation they oversee. To keep is to protect fruit producers from internal and external threats such as pestilence, fire, floods, storms, earthquakes, disease, bandits, etc. For example, military members swear to protect the Constitution from all threats, foreign and domestic. Protecting a thing or a life is all-encompassing. A key to keeping or protecting our portion of creation is to ensure the things and people we interact with are healthy enough to provide self-protection; thus, if we tend properly, our need to protect lowers. But if we fail to protect, there will be nothing to tend.

God had the man name the beasts of the garden to exercise authority over the other living things. Having authority gave the man the right to make necessary tending and keeping decisions about the other living creatures in the portion of creation he was made steward. Authority doesn't mean you have the best ideas for doing something; it means that the buck stops with you. If something in your area of responsibility fails, you are the one to correct the problem.

Having authority doesn't mean those you lead will be obedient. Obedience is a second-to-second choice all image-bearers have. The people for whom you are responsible and over whom you have authority will not always be obedient to your leadership. When they are not, remember that we are not always obedient to God's will, even though He is perfect.

Jesus showed unconditional love to His followers. He died for the sins of all people, even those who rejected Him. Unconditional love for those we are charged with is what God requires from His steward, along with a willingness to use the best methods for tending and keeping. Even then, we might experience rejection from those we lead, just as our Lord and Savior experienced. Let's look at what happens to the tending, keeping, and exercising authority tasks when a steward chooses disobedience.

Disobedient Stewardship

Simply stated, choosing disobedience to God is a selfish act. It occurs when individuals choose to determine what is best for themselves rather than following God's will. The problem with self-determination is that we don't have all the data. We don't know how everything works inside or outside of us.

Newton's third law states that for every action in nature, there is an opposite and equal reaction. We could explore the meaning of Newton's law further, but a summation of the quantum mechanics involved in the law is that we are all connected in more ways than we fully understand. Because we are all connected, stewards who choose to disobey God produce one of two opposing ethical codes.

The first code is associated with deliberately choosing to act against God's will out of a willingness to limit or harm others in order to attain what the person wants. This is the choice of the predator, the bully, or the despot.

The second code on the opposite end of the disobedience spectrum is associated with choosing to act against God's will out of a belief that the person's actions are of no consequence to others. This is the choice of the naïve, the ignorant, and the thoughtless. We will examine how those opposing codes of ethics manifest themselves in disobedient stewardship.

Disobedience in Tending

When a person is disobedient to God out of a willingness to limit or harm others deliberately, the person doesn't tend; the person **takes**. Imagine a large garden that produces enough food to feed everyone. The taker either collects all of the food or the best food and forces everyone else to pay for what he has taken, increasing his power over the garden. A person who takes instead of tends does not believe in the inherent goodness of God. The person believes that he is more important than others and that other image-bearers are less deserving than he is. This kind of disobedience displays itself as someone who does not ensure that other image-bearers are treated equally and fairly. In a family dynamic, this is the husband or dad who believes the family is supposed to take care of him, rather than his taking care of them.

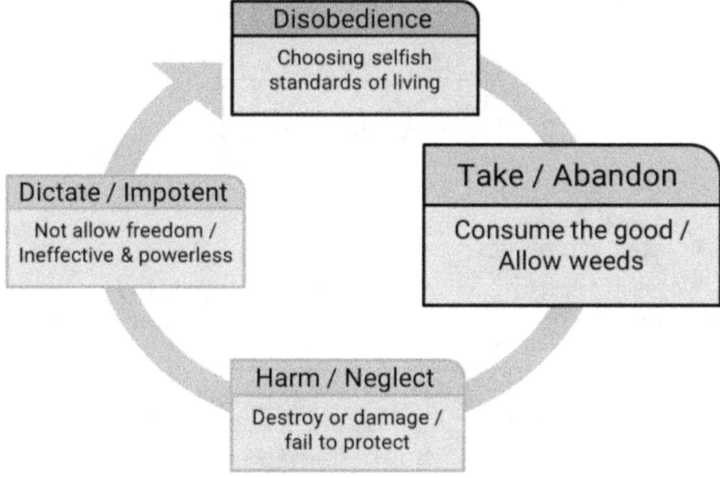

Figure 4 - Effects of Disobedience on Tending

The other disobedient choice when it comes to tending is to **abandon**, and we'll use our garden scenario again as an example. The person who is supposed to tend the garden instead abandons it, letting weeds populate and deteriorate what God has placed in his care. The abandonment forces someone else to take on the responsibility of cleaning the garden. This is what happens to wives whose husbands leave them, or to children whose earthly fathers refuse to be in their lives. The image-bearers who are supposed to be nurtured and cared for by one of God's stewards are abandoned and left to feed themselves.

Disobedience in Keeping

Regarding keeping or protecting, the two sides of the disobedience spectrum are harming and neglecting. Harming is the intentional decision to damage the portion of God's creation over which the steward is placed. The choice to **harm** the portion of God's creation a steward oversees comes from the ethical code that God is not good, and every man must look out for himself. When it comes to other image-bearers, harming can take the form of physically, psychologically, or emotionally damaging other people, which, of course, is against God's will.

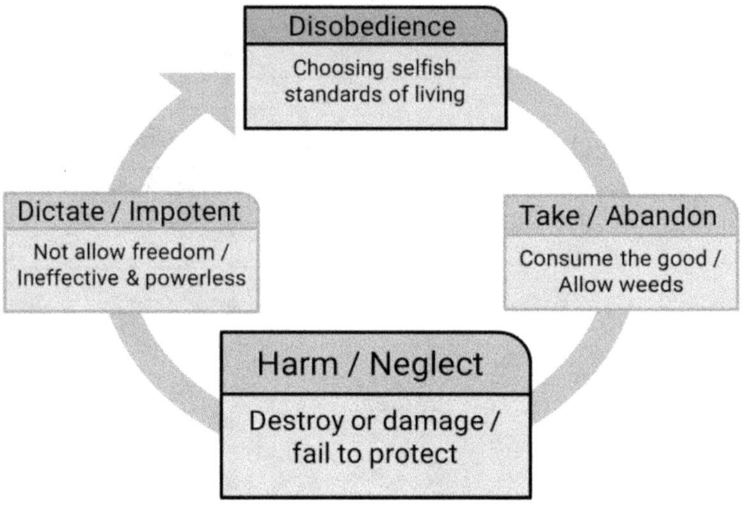

Figure 5 - Effects of Disobedience on Keeping

Neglect is displayed by the steward who believes what he does is not important. It is an act of thoughtlessness, naivety, or ignorance of danger. The neglectful steward may not believe he is failing to protect appropriately. He might not know something is wrong out of ignorance. Neglect happens when we fail to pay attention to the details. It occurs when we are self-absorbed and fail to attend to the needs of others. According to Philippians 2:3, we are to "Do nothing from selfish ambition or conceit, but in humility count others more significant than" ourselves. A neglectful steward invites the dangers of this world into the lives of those he is supposed to protect.

Disobedience in Exercising Authority

Human societies—from the family unit to large-scale governments—require leadership. Every structure has a leader, and leadership vacuums will not remain empty. The right to name the other creatures means man was given the stewardship task of exercising leadership authority in God's creation. Disobedience in exercising authority produces one of two outcomes: a dictatorship or chaos. The stewards who **dictate** are men who abuse their positions of authority out of a belief that they alone can operate their accumulated power. These men falsely believe that their power will shelter them and protect them from the evils of this world. At their core, they fail to trust in God appropriately and believe they have to limit the freedoms of other image-bearers to maintain authority over the structure they lead.

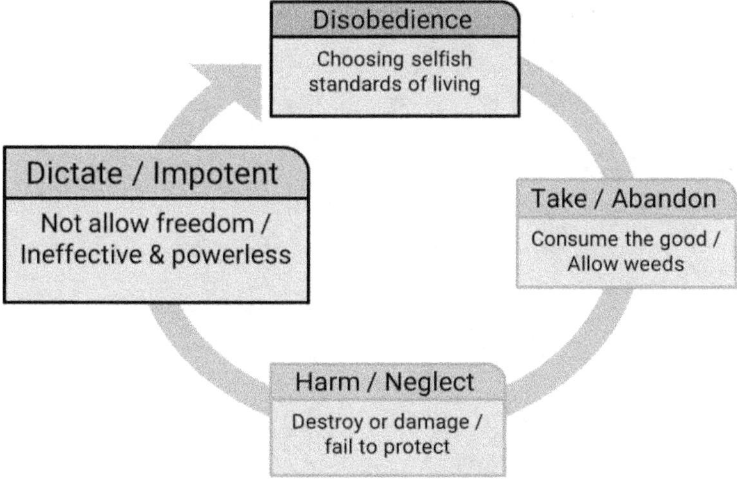

Figure 6 - Effects of Disobedience on Exercising Authority

The flip side of the dictator is the **impotent** man. This is the steward who does not understand God's command to lead what has been placed in his care. The impotent steward is indecisive, ineffective, and refuses to accept responsibility for the portion of God's creation that he has been given. The problem with the impotent man is God's creation is alive and ever-changing, regardless of his willingness to take charge or not. When the steward fails to exercise authority properly, his portion of God's creation experiences chaos because of a leadership vacuum. Chaos prevents those in the steward's sphere of influence from being properly tended or protected. The impotent steward invites sin into his portion of creation and allows it to flourish because he cannot or will not exercise leadership.

Summary

Let's leave this lesson by reminding ourselves what good stewardship looks like. It begins with acknowledging that God is who He says He is, and nothing belongs to us except our choices and actions. By hearing from God and submitting to His will, we allow Him to lead us into the successful stewardship of the portion of creation He has placed us over. Failing to obey the Creator and Owner of what we are to steward jeopardizes our privilege of stewardship. God could take our portion away from us and, at the very least, will require an accounting of what He has placed in our hands.

Lesson Application - Which of the three stewardship tasks (tend, keep, and exercise authority), all conducted while in obedience to God's commands, do you best perform? What evidence do you have for that belief?

Lesson 19

A Warrior's Mindset

Context

The previous lesson examined the negative impact disobedience has on the stewardship tasks of tending, protecting, and exercising authority. To be a good steward of our portion of God's creation, we must remind ourselves that we are born into and live in a war zone where spiritual forces battle for the souls of humanity. A warrior's mindset is essential for stewarding God's creation obediently.

The Battlefield's Opponents

In John 14:15, our Lord Jesus Christ called for our obedience. As Lord, He is our battlefield commander, and three opponents threaten our obedience to Him. The first is God's enemy and his army of fallen angels, who hate God and seek the death and destruction of God's image-bearers. The second opponent is this world, which propagates the enemy's lies to tempt image-bearers to sin and separation from our Creator. The third is our natural heart and flesh that want to give in to temptation and oppose God's Spirit. A biblical story found in all four Gospels helps explain why the three opponents threaten our choice to be the men God created us to be (Matthew 26:57-75, Mark 14:53-65, Luke 22:66-23:25, and John 18:19-24).

Following His arrest, Jesus was taken to the Jewish priests, elders, and scribes who tried to find a legitimate reason for condemning Him to death. Ultimately, blasphemy was the only charge brought against Jesus. The Jewish leaders who had the training and education to recognize fulfilled prophecy condemned to death the Scripture's promised Messiah because He told them the truth, that He was the Son of God. Jesus was condemned for the truth about who He was.

Men, the world, and those "of the world" don't want you to express and live out your true identity—a son of the Father, a brother to Jesus, and a vessel of the Holy Spirit who stewards a portion of God's creation. Those of the world want you to be like them, a fraud, a fake, someone who hides behind a mask and lies. John 3:19 tells us that those of the world want to live in darkness. They do not want to be exposed by God's light. Worldly people have chosen to deny God's truth and do not want to be reminded of their decision. They rejected God's grace and are compelled by their sin to bury the truth.

As men of God, we must obediently stand against living in lies. We know they only generate a more chaotic and confusing battlefield. When we choose disobedience to our Lord, our true enemy heaps more lies upon us, such as "you're no good," "you're not saved," "you're a liar," "you're an adulterer," "you're a hypocrite," "you're a murderer," etc. Those lies are intended to make us doubt our standing with Jesus. They create confusion, eventually leading to doubt. Doubt erodes confidence in Jesus as Lord and Savior, which leads to more sin. Never forget that we sin because we give up on God, not because God gives up on us.

James discusses this in verses twelve through eighteen in the opening chapter of his book.

> Blessed is the man who remains steadfast under trial, for when he has stood the test he will receive the crown of life, which God has promised to those who love him. Let no one say when he is tempted, 'I am being tempted by God,' for God cannot

> be tempted with evil, and he himself tempts no one. But each person is tempted when he is lured and enticed by his own desire. Then desire when it has conceived gives birth to sin, and sin when it is fully grown brings forth death. Do not be deceived, my beloved brothers. Every good gift and every perfect gift is from above, coming down from the Father of lights, with whom there is no variation or shadow due to change. Of his own will he brought us forth by the word of truth, that we should be a kind of firstfruits of his creatures. (James 1:12-18)

God does not tempt, and He is the One who has given us anything good we have in our lives.

A Warrior's Mindset

A warrior's mindset begins with knowing that God has placed us in stewardship authority over a portion of His creation, tasking us with nurturing and protecting what is His while combating the spiritual forces set against Him. We can take solace because we know the One who placed us here is Himself a warrior. Following the crossing of the Red Sea, where Pharaoh and his army were wiped out, the men of Israel sang a song of joy to the Lord. Exodus 15:3 provides one of the lines of the song, "The LORD is a warrior; Yahweh is His name."

Our Warrior LORD has empowered us with His Spirit to overcome the obstacles we face in our stewardship tasks. We must decide to be dependable stewards who will always fight for God's Kingdom. We know we have already been forgiven because Jesus took our sins to the cross nearly 2,000 years ago. We should not live in shame or regret.

We cannot allow the enemy's lies to lead us into doubting the LORD our God. We know the world and its followers will try to stop us from being the warriors God calls us to be. When we lose a fight—and we will—we know that we must get back in the fight because the war is not over. God wants us to steward His creation successfully. He does not want us to wallow in our losses and pay homage to the enemy's lies, particularly since Jesus has already paid the price for those losses.

According to Psalm 115:3, 1 Chronicles 29:11, and Daniel 4:35, God is the sovereign power of everything. He has absolute power, and if He says we are cleansed of sin, we should behave like it. Genesis 2:7, Job 33:4, and Ephesians 1:11 substantiate that God created us and gave us life to do His will.

The truth is we exist to serve God, and a warrior chooses to live in that truth at all times because that truth is what sets us free of sin, as stated in John 8:32 and Galatians 5:1. A warrior chooses to stand in the truth even though sometimes his stance will cause a fight. Second Timothy 3:12 states, "Indeed, all who want to live in a godly way in Christ Jesus will be persecuted." First Peter 3:14-15 tells us, "But even if you should suffer for righteousness, you are blessed. And do not fear their intimidation, and do not be in dread, but in your hearts honor Christ the Lord as holy, always being prepared to make a defense to anyone who asks you for a reason for the hope that is in you; yet do it with gentleness and respect."

A warrior does what's right even when it costs him because he knows he has already won the prize of eternal salvation. According to Ecclesiastes 5:15, Job 1:21, Psalm 49:17, and 1 Timothy 6:7, we enter this world naked and will leave this world naked. There is only one action, decision, or choice we are all forced to make in this world, and that is determining where our souls will go when our bodies die. Beyond acceptance into God's family and kingdom, what else is to be gained from this world?

A Warrior's Responsibilities

We have explored the important characteristic of a warrior—truth. A warrior for God will always stand in the truth. A warrior does this because the enemy and his forces always lie because they are born of lies. One of the truths we stand in is—wherever you are, there you are. You may not want to be where you are, but that doesn't mean you get to make someone else responsible for your condition.

As His image-bearer, God gave you the power to choose. As an adult, you are responsible for your conditions no matter who or what played a part in you being where you are, so don't blame God for anything negative in your life. James 1:17 and Matthew 7:11 tell us that He only gives good gifts. Also, don't blame another image-bearer for the negative things in your life. Romans 2:1 tells us we are no better than anyone else.

The war into which we are born produces casualties and death, and the smallest, most innocuous decision we make could unknowingly lead to destruction. We are not promised rose gardens. Instead, in Genesis 3:17-19, God promised a cursed ground that brings forth thorns and thistles that we will have to work around to eat, so we can one day return to the very dust He created us from. Men, life is hard. It becomes even harder when we fail to accept responsibility for our lives.

Accept the good and bad in your life. Maintain the good in your life and fix the bad. Live a life of no excuses. When you make a mistake, own up to it and fix it. Don't say you're not capable of fixing the bad or that you don't have time to fix the bad. Did God give you a brain and a body? Does His Spirit live in your heart?

You may lack knowledge and experience, but you do not lack the capability of stewarding what He has given you. It may take you the remainder of your existence in this world to accomplish what God has placed on you, or for you to correct a mistake you made. For example, while we don't know the exact timeframe, it took about 100 years for Noah to build the ark, according to Genesis 6:14 through 7:1. God gave Noah a momentous task, which he accepted for nearly a century.

No matter what, don't take a coward's way out. Accept responsibility for the life God has given you, live in obedience to His will, and correct the mistakes you make to the best of your ability for however long you have left in this world. Getting right with Him is the only mission we have in this world.

Men, the people with whom God has placed you, or will place you need to see a man of God operating from the truth and for the truth. They need to witness integrity, honesty, decency, kindness, and virtue. They need to see selflessness in action. They need to see love. They need to know there are men who will seek their good at all times regardless of what they have done or will do. They need to know they are not alone and be inspired. This world contains lost and weak people who need to be inspired by our example as God's warriors. Even warriors can be inspired by the actions of other warriors. As righteous warriors, we can gain ground for God's Kingdom while bringing other men alongside to help us.

Because we are God's warriors, we need to have an offensive mindset rather than a defensive one. We should be proactive, not reactive. We should act in faith, not in fear. In fact, a good defensive strategy is to put the enemy on his heels. A good offense is sometimes the best defense; simply stated, we need to be a danger to the enemy's plans.

Fearlessness

Men, we have the living God inside of us. That very fact makes us dangerous to the enemy who withers before God. He has no chance against the Holy Spirit residing in us. But the enemy knows weakness when he sees it. Like a wild animal, he can smell fear and has no choice but to exploit our weaknesses in an effort to destroy us. The enemy doesn't feel sorry for us. Why should he? We are image-bearers, designed to be closer to the Creator than he was.

He will kill us if he can. If he cannot kill us, he will drag us through the mud and spit on us while he's doing it, even if you're eternally saved. As long as we remain on our bellies, wallowing in our excrement, we can't be the salt and light of this world (Matthew 5:13-16). We are of no eternal consequence to the image-bearers with whom we come into contact.

There is no point in getting mad at the enemy and his forces. They are simply behaving in accordance with what they are: evil. Their attacks are not personal; they simply hate God. Expect to be attacked and prepare accordingly. Become part of the solution instead of part of the problem.

We should be dangerous but under the absolute control of our commander, Lord Jesus Christ. We can be dangerous in making our portion of God's creation healthy and fruitful. We can be dangerous in avoiding the enemy's temptation traps. We can be dangerous in spreading the good news of salvation through Jesus Christ and discipling others to follow the Way (Acts 9:2, 19:9, 23, 22:4, and 24:14, 22). Our actions speak louder than words, and we should set the example for others to follow.

In the opening chapter of 2nd Timothy, Paul reminds us, "For God gave us a spirit not of fear but of power and love and self-control." As God's stewards, we must choose to live for truth out of obedience to become warriors for God's Kingdom.

Lesson Application

Men, there will be times when it feels like everything is against us when nothing makes sense. In those moments, we need to have something to focus on when we are in the fight. Some easy things to always remember are:

- ☐ God loves you and wants a relationship with you.
- ☐ God is the only good that we will ever know.

- ☐ God never lies.
- ☐ God always fulfills His promises.

Write down at least one Bible verse on which you can focus during the chaos of spiritual warfare.

Lesson 20

Woman

Context

The previous lesson introduced the mindset of a warrior, a mindset built on the fundamental truth that men are designed to steward God's creation. Genesis 2:15-20 tells us God commanded man to work, keep, and exercise authority in obedience to His will over a portion of creation. A good steward actively and, when necessary, aggressively defends his portion of creation. And because we exist in a spiritual war zone, we must be prepared for aggressive action. A warrior-minded steward fearlessly stands on truth, posing a dangerous threat to potential enemies who use lies "to steal, kill, and destroy" (John 10:10).

Seeking Peace

A good steward does not seek confrontation; he seeks peace. David, who is perhaps the Bible's greatest example of a warrior, states the relationship between security and peace in Psalm 122:6-9. "Pray for the peace of Jerusalem! / "May they be secure who love you! / Peace be within your walls / and security within your towers!" / For my brothers and companions' sake / I will say, "Peace be within you!" / For the sake of the house of the Lord our God, / I will seek your good."

While a good steward seeks peace, he must be capable of exercising the authority needed to keep or protect his portion of God's creation, allowing him to work and nurture the portion in accordance with God's command. Sometimes, exercising authority requires war, but we should cultivate peaceful relationships because sustained growth is practically impossible during war. Peace begins with getting right with God, and we know the only way to get right with God is to accept and believe in Jesus as Lord and Savior. Once we have peace with God, we receive His supernatural ability to establish and maintain peaceful relationships with others by His Spirit.

Peace with God and other image-bearers is not just good stewardship but a command from Jesus in Matthew 22:37-40. "'You shall love the Lord your God with all your heart, and with all your soul, and with all your mind.' This is the great and foremost commandment. The second is like it, 'You shall love your neighbor as yourself.' Upon these two commandments hang the whole Law and the Prophets."

Honoring the command from our Lord Jesus means we do not instigate fights with other people. We should seek to unify people, not divide them. Numerous verses substantiate this claim, including:

- Psalm 34:14, "Turn away from evil and do good; seek peace and pursue it."
- Proverbs 17:14, "The beginning of strife is like letting out water, so quit before the quarrel breaks out."
- Matthew 5:9, "Blessed are the peacemakers, for they will be called sons of God."
- Romans 12:18, "If possible, so far as it depends on you, live peaceably with all."
- First Corinthians 1:10, "I appeal to you, brothers, by the name of our Lord Jesus Christ, that all of you agree, and that there

be no divisions among you, but that you be united in the same mind and the same judgment."

- Hebrews 12:14, "Strive for peace with everyone, and for the holiness without which no one will see the Lord."
- First Peter 3:8, "Finally, all of you, have unity of mind, sympathy, brotherly love, a tender heart, and a humble mind."

Undoubtedly, God commands us to seek a peaceful relationship with Him then with the other image-bearers with whom we exist. In prioritizing our relationships, most men's second most important relationship is with the woman in their lives. Genesis 2:18 provides the reason why: "Then the Lord God said, 'It is not good that the man should be alone; I will make him a helper fit for him.'" This lesson introduces woman, the image-bearer created specifically for us. Woman was the final act in God's creation.

Woman, Creation's Crowning Jewel

Woman is the icing on a cake, the cream and sugar in a coffee, the bow on a present. Genesis 1:31 tells us that after the woman was created, God said His work became "very good." And Genesis 2:2 tells us that God rested once the woman was created. A truthful statement is that woman was the crowning jewel of God's creation.

She was created to be beautiful (Genesis 12:11 & 24:16; 2 Samuel 11:2; Esther 2:7; Song of Solomon 1:15 & 4:7). She is soft, curvy, and smooth. She smells nice. Her voice and touch can soothe. She is noticed when she walks into the room. Her smile makes our hearts flutter. She is desired. She is wanted. When we think of beauty, we think of the woman. And nothing compares to the beauty of a woman who willingly gives herself to her man. She can love with everything she has. Her love has no boundaries. It can be reckless and consuming. Wars have been fought over her. Promises are made because of her.

Works of art have been made to honor her. God designed woman specifically for man; man cannot help but want her.

Scientifically, women are different than men in every physical detail. The National Institute of Health states that the differences between males and females are expressed at the cellular level. In other words, a cell's DNA—the smallest substance we can measure—is expressed as male or female. Every physical trait of a woman is non-male.

Generally speaking, women also think and feel differently from men. Looking good is usually more important to a woman than actually being good. Women are concerned about form while men are concerned about function. A woman's emotions tend to have a wider variance than a man's. Sometimes, those emotions go too far; they get the best of her, leaving her vulnerable to getting hurt.

Even though women are different than men, they innately understand their need for a man's strength, just as we need their beauty. In Genesis 2:24, God commands the husband and wife to become one. Similar to the Holy Trinity forming one God, a husband and wife make one version of flesh. Marriage was intended to be an unbreakable, exclusive, lifelong union. Termination of marriage was not considered before sin came into the world (Genesis 3). The Bible teaches that all instances of separation and divorce were because of sin. See Deuteronomy 24:1-4; Ezra 9-10; Malachi 2:14; Matthew 5:31-32; and Luke 16:18.

Why Woman Was Created

God created woman because it was not good for man to be alone. Additionally, woman was created to help man steward God's creation. At her core, she wants to fulfill the task for which God designed her. She wants to be with the man and help him.

The English Standard Version (ESV) of Genesis 2:18 states, "Then the Lord God said, 'It is not good that the man should be alone; I will make him a helper fit for him.'" The last phrase of this verse, "a helper fit for him," is translated differently in other versions, such as:

- a helper corresponding to him (Christian Standard Bible, CSB)
- a helper that is perfect for him (Contemporary English Bible, CEB)
- the companion he needs, one just right for him (Easy to Read Version ERV)
- a suitable companion to help him (Good News Translation, GNT)
- a helper as his complement (Holman Christian Standard Bible, HCSB)
- a helper as his counterpart (Lexham English Bible, LEB)
- a companion for him, a helper suited to his needs (The Living Bible, TLB)
- a helper who is just right for him (New Living Translation, NLT)
- a helper suitable for him (New International Version, NIV)
- a helper comparable to him (New King James Version, NKJV)

Scripture surrounding Genesis 2:18 contextualizes and deepens our understanding of why God made woman. Verse fifteen states, "The LORD God took the man and put him in the garden of Eden to work it and keep it." This verse contains God's first two commands to the steward of His garden: work, which is also translated as tend or nurture, and keep or protect.

Verses sixteen and seventeen contain God's third command: obey. Those verses state, "And the LORD God commanded the man, saying,

'You may surely eat of every tree of the garden, but of the tree of the knowledge of good and evil you shall not eat, for in the day that you eat of it you shall surely die.'" Three commands to man occur before Genesis 2:18 when God says He will make a helper for the man.

God's fourth command to his steward was to exercise authority over the other creatures in the garden in verses nineteen and the first portion of verse twenty, "Now out of the ground the LORD God had formed every beast of the field and every bird of the heavens and brought them to the man to see what he would call them. And whatever the man called every living creature, that was its name. The man gave names to all livestock and to the birds of the heavens and to every beast of the field." The last sentence in verse twenty states, "But for Adam, there was not found a helper fit for him."

Verses twenty-one and twenty-two of Genesis 2 show us how God made woman. They state, "So the LORD God caused a deep sleep to fall upon the man, and while he slept, took one of his ribs and closed up its place with flesh. And the rib that the Lord God had taken from the man he made into a woman and brought her to the man."

Origin and Identity

God created woman from man, which is different from how He created man. Genesis 2:7 states, "Then the LORD God formed the man of dust from the ground and breathed into his nostrils the breath of life, and the man became a living creature." God created man from dust. How God created man and woman is an important distinction to keep in mind because it explains where we get our identity. Whom you identify as right now has a beginning story; it has an origin. Your given name, your family name, and where you are from are all used to explain your identity.

God breathes life into all people, and all of us bear His image. The man comes from the dust of the ground God created, while the woman comes from man. In fact, the very name *woman* means "from man."

According to a professor at the Israel Bible Center, the Hebrew word for man is "ish" (אִישׁ), and for woman is "isha" (אִשָּׁה). While these two words, "ish" and "isha," sound similar, they do not share a common Hebrew root word. The word "ish" comes from a root word meaning "strength," while "isha" comes from a root word meaning "fragile."[4] This helps explain the idea of a woman as the "weaker vessel," as stated in 1 Peter 3:7, and also why women look for men who possess protective strength.

Another Hebrew Studies organization claims the English translation of God making a woman from a man's rib is inaccurate. The site claims the real Hebraic meaning is that God took a side from the man, or He split the man in half to make a woman.[5] If this claim is correct, woman is the other half of man. She is the necessary component for a man to become a full image-bearer. Likewise, a woman needs a man to become the full image-bearer she was created to be. Further, it requires a man and a woman to fulfill God's command in Genesis 1:29, which is to "be fruitful and multiply and fill the earth."

Summarizing God's commands to man and the creation of woman begins with God placing man in the garden to tend and keep it in Gen 2:15. Second, God told the man to obey one command in Gen 2:16-17. Third, He told the man to name the other creatures to exercise authority in Gen 2:19-20. Finally, the woman was created in Gen 2:21.

Make no mistake. While woman is equal to man, God made man responsible for His creation. The woman was created to help with the man's stewardship responsibility. She was uniquely designed to share in the ways in which a man has a responsibility to God's creation.

---

4 Lizorkin-Eyzenberg, Eli. "The Essential Role of a Biblical Woman." Israel Bible Center. April 27, 2018. https://www.facebook.com/IsraelBibleCenter/posts/435650093545221/

5 Bentorah, Chaim. "Hebrew Word Study – Woman." Chaim Bentorah Biblical Hebrew Studies. May 1, 2018. https://www.chaimbentorah.com/2018/05/hebrew-word-study-woman/

For example, let's look at God's command to tend His creation. Tending has numerous synonyms, but let's use farming and nurturing as examples. Generally, men are thought of as better farmers while women are generally thought of as better nurturers; thus, sometimes, the stewardship task of tending is better suited for a man, and sometimes it is better suited for a woman.

How about the command to keep? Keeping is roughly equivalent to protecting. Generally, men are considered better overall protectors than women because of physical strength; however, the wide use and understanding of the expression "mama bear" indicate that women can be highly protective of their children. So, sometimes the man is a better keeper, and sometimes the woman is better.

Obeying God's commands is something to which both men and women are expected to adhere, and both can have a positive or negative influence on other image-bearers. A wider divergence is seen in the stewardship task of naming or exercising authority. Undoubtedly, women have proven to be leaders who effectively exercise authority within God's will. While recent societal changes have encouraged more women to take leadership positions, men still constitute the majority of positions where authority is exercised. Additionally, all or nearly all societies acknowledge men as the family leader because most women take their husbands' last names.

Men, our primary relationship is with God. According to Matthew 22:37, peace with God occurs when we obey His will out of love for Him. The second most important relationship is with our wives, who make us complete image bearers while helping us fulfill our stewardship responsibilities. According to Matthew 22:39, peace with our wives begins when we love them as ourselves.

Lesson Application - In "Lesson 10 - God's Stewards," you listed areas of stewardship over which God has placed you in authority.

If you are married, explain one or more of the stewardship tasks your wife helps you with in detail. How does she assist you in stewarding what God has placed under your authority?

If you are not married, what qualities should you look for in a future wife to assist you in the successful stewardship of your portion of God's creation?

Lesson 21

The Wife

Context

In the last lesson, we introduced the woman to the Discipled Warriors study program. From Genesis 2:18, we know God created women to be our companions who assist us in fulfilling our stewardship tasks. The companionship of a woman is so close that she and her man become "one flesh" (Genesis 2:24). Because of that proximal relationship, the woman God places in our care becomes our second priority in relational peace. This lesson continues the discussion on women to help us better understand how to have peace with our wives.

Sex

Wives are the second most important relationship for most men because most adult males will get married; however, some men have not yet married, and some are divorced or widowed and could remarry. There are other categories of unmarried men, and the sexual activity of those men is the reason for their singleness.

Some single men do not want to commit to only one woman out of the preference for having multiple sexual partners. Some men sexually desire other men and choose not to be married to a woman.

Some men—like Catholic priests—choose not to be married and abstain from sex. Some men do not have sexual desires and choose to live without a wife; 1 Corinthians 7:6-9 suggests the Apostle Paul was such a man. For the majority of men, marriage is how we fulfill our desire for sexual intimacy.

By itself, sex is not a sin. Like money, guns, or nuclear power, sex is not evil, and the desire for sex is not wrong. Now, sex outside of the marital union is a sin, but sex within a marriage is a gift from God. God designed us to have sex. Without sex, God's command in Genesis 1:28 to "Be fruitful and multiply, and fill the earth, and subdue it" cannot be fulfilled.

The last lesson went to great lengths in describing how God designed women to be desirable for sex. A beautiful woman quickens the pulse of any man she is near. Her smile, words, and touch cause the cognitive function of most men to decrease substantially. Most men have a strong desire to bond with desirable women sexually. The mere opportunity for sexual intimacy drives the actions of most men, causing us to perform incredible works in an attempt to woo a beauty to bed with us.

Without a doubt, the desire for sexual bonding with another image-bearer is genuine, even for women. That desire is particularly strong when a person is young, energetic, and beginning to realize his or her adult identity.

A husband and wife should have sex. Like good food, hot showers, and warm beds, the enjoyment of marital sex is a God-given gift. Song of Solomon 4 and Proverbs 5 contain Scriptural passages endorsing marital sex.

How men and women think about sex is generally different. I once heard an elderly woman summarize how men and women view sex differently. She said, "Men have sex to feel good. Women need to feel good to have sex." While the woman's quote may not be accurate in all circumstances, keep what she said in mind the next time you wonder why your wife isn't as sexually motivated as you want her to be. Not only does a woman need to feel desired and wanted by her man, but she also needs to feel good about herself.

For those of us who have been married for more than a few years, we understand that sex is not the primary reason why we stay married. We know that many other things become prioritized over sex as a marriage matures. Even as a marriage matures, sexual intimacy between a husband and wife should remain. Biblically, sexual relations should only occur between a husband and wife. Verses that substantiate this stance include 1 Corinthian 7:2, which states, "But because of the temptation to sexual immorality, each man should have his own wife and each woman her own husband," and Hebrews 13:4, which states, "Let marriage be held in honor among all, and let the marriage bed be undefiled, for God will judge the sexually immoral and adulterous."

Sex outside of marriage is where we run into problems. In God's Word, sex outside of marriage—adultery—is always a sin. Exodus 20:14 & Deuteronomy 5:18, "You shall not commit adultery." Proverbs 6:32 says, "He who commits adultery lacks sense; / he who does it destroys himself." First Corinthians 6:18 says, "Flee from sexual immorality. Every other sin a person commits is outside the body, but the sexually immoral person sins against his own body." Galatians 5:19 says, "Now the works of the flesh are evident: sexual immorality, impurity, and sensuality." Ephesians 5:5, "For you may be sure of this, that everyone who is sexually immoral or impure…has no inheritance in the kingdom of Christ and God."

Pornography

Adultery—or sex outside of marriage—includes pornography. In Matthew 5:27-28, Jesus stated, "You have heard that it was said, 'You shall not commit adultery.' But I say to you that everyone who looks at a woman with lustful intent has already committed adultery with her in his heart."

One of the enemy's best temptation devices in today's world is pornography. Viewing and masturbating to pornography is adultery. It is sexually immoral just like the acts of homosexuality or bestiality. There is no way around this fact.

Pornography is pervasive. It is a $100-billion-per-year industry that nearly twenty percent of American males routinely use. Sadly, these percentages are no different between men who identify as Christians versus men who identify as non-Christians. Porn taps into the same brain centers as drugs, alcohol, and gambling. This means pornography is highly addictive. And, like all other negative addictions, pornography's harm isn't limited to the viewer.

Addiction to pornography can cause a person to not want sexual intimacy with another person. It can lead to erectile dysfunction, a disorder that today is found in one-third (thirty-three percent) of men under the age of thirty. In 1960, only one percent of men under thirty had erectile dysfunction. While porn cannot be said to be the causative agent for erectile dysfunction, the increase over the past sixty years makes it corollary. Further proof is the amount of advertisements for erectile dysfunction medications. Doesn't it seem like there are an inordinate number of ads that focus on improving men's ability to have sex? That industry is selling products to someone.

The addiction to pornographic masturbation produces feelings of depression and loneliness among men. Clearly, pornography has some real negative effects, but it gets worse. Pornographic addiction is definitely a way the enemy gains strongholds in men's hearts. Like other strongholds, pornography leads to further depravity, which is exactly what the enemy wants. What pornography ultimately causes is seeing other people—particularly women—as sexual objects only, no longer as people. Seeing people as objects and not as image-bearers of God fosters evil.

Research has shown that pornography addiction is the gateway to physical adultery and pedophilia or sexual relations with children.

Seeing people as objects is how the indiscriminate murder we see in our society is fostered. Seeing people as objects is how genocide—or the eradication of a people—has occurred in the past and continues to occur today. When we no longer see people as God's image-bearers, depravity and evil are sure to follow.

Understandably, pornography is a subject we don't like to discuss. It is embarrassing to discuss its struggles openly. If it's something you struggle with, I'm going to point you to a source I trust. Search for Dr. John Foubert. John is a credible researcher whom I have worked with in the past and trust as a follower of Jesus. While his book *How Pornography Harms* (2017) is a bit dated, it is a good place to start.[6]

Marriage Dynamics

God designed women and men to be united in marital relationships. Trust, communication, boundaries, conflict, and emotions all play roles in relationship dynamics, and the Bible informs us how to maintain relationships. Jesus's Great Commandment in Matthew 22:39 tells us to love our neighbor as ourselves. The golden rule, which is stated in Matthew 7:12 and Luke 6:31, tells us that we should treat others as we want to be treated.

Ephesians 5:22-33 provides the clearest statement on the dynamics between a husband and wife. That passage states that most husbands struggle to love their wives unconditionally and that most wives struggle to allow their husbands to be the head of the household. The remainder of this lesson will focus on those two dynamics from a man's perspective: loving your wife unconditionally and encouraging your wife to submit to your leadership willingly.

---

[6] Foubert, John. *How Pornography Harms: What Today's Teens, Young Adults, Parents, and Pastors Need to Know*. LifeRich Publishing. 2017.

Unconditional Love

Colossians 3:19 and 1 Peter 3:7 encourage men to love their wives. Ephesians 5:25 states, "Husbands, love your wives, as Christ loved the Church and gave himself up for her." This begs the question: How did Christ love the Church?

Ephesians 5:2 tells us, "Christ loved us and gave himself up for us as a fragrant offering and sacrifice to God." Romans 5:8 adds, "But God shows his love for us in that while we were still sinners, Christ died for us." Jesus demonstrated His love for the Church by sacrificing His life to pay for our sins—even though we did nothing to deserve His sacrifice. Without His sacrifice, members of the Church had no chance of an eternal relationship with God. We could not have *shalom*.

A term we can use to describe Christ's love for the Church is unconditional. Unconditional love means doing what is best for another person, regardless of whether you think the person deserves your efforts or not. Unconditional love is selflessness. The natural man is selfish, but because we are a new creation where God's Holy Spirit resides, we can demonstrate supernatural, unconditional love to our wives.

For many years, I did not understand that my job as a husband was to demonstrate unconditional love to my wife. Because of my lack of understanding, my marriage was on the brink of divorce at least every couple of months. My marriage strengthened once I realized my job as a husband was to choose unconditional love for my wife. Proof of our strengthened marriage is that my wife demonstrably wants to spend time with me, and our disagreements no longer broach the idea of divorce. My choice to love her unconditionally became easier once I accepted that she was God's daughter. He gave His daughter to me as a wife to love, cherish, and care for in this world.

Leadership

The second relationship dynamic between husbands and wives is stated by Ephesians 5:22, which says, "Wives, submit to your own husbands, as to the Lord," and 1 Peter 3:1, "Wives be subject to your own husband." As husbands, we must demonstrate effective leadership to encourage our wives to submit willingly to our stewardship authority.

Effective leaders accept the blame for failures and give credit for successes. When things go well, good leaders complement members of the team. When things go badly, good leaders state what they did wrong. This is not an easy task, but it is a standard that all good leaders accept and improve upon with practice. In a marriage relationship, husbands are the leaders; thus, when something negative occurs, husbands must accept responsibility. Similarly, when things go well, a good husband will credit his wife—and mean it.

Our identity as family leaders means we must make all decisions with our wives' safety and benefit in mind. Not every choice a husband makes will be good, but our wives need to trust that we will make decisions that benefit them. They need to know that they are safe within our sphere of control.

Being the marital leader doesn't mean the husband is the only decision-maker or that the wife isn't more equipped to make better decisions than her husband in some areas. Like you, she is an image-bearer and has the ability to choose. Sometimes her choices are bad. If she makes a decision without your input that irreparably harms the marriage or family, then she will have to answer to God for that decision. But a spiritually mature wife will seek her husband's input before making weighty decisions. If your wife does make a poor decision, remember that two wrongs don't make a right. As God's appointed steward, you must make decisions in her best interests regardless of the decisions she makes.

Gender Identity

Men and women have different marital roles because of their different origins. The first man was made from the dust of the ground that God created (Genesis 2:7). Thus, the identity of men originates from the Creator.

The origin of women is different, meaning they have different roles in marriage. The first woman was made from the first man (Genesis 2:22). Thus, the identity of women originates from the men in their lives.

This does not mean a woman cannot have a personal relationship with God. As an image bearer, a woman is expected to have a direct relationship with our Lord and Savior. Because a woman's identity originates from the primary man in their life, a woman's husband greatly influences how the woman sees herself.

Because a man's identity originates from the Creator, men can choose to see themselves as God sees them or can allow their wives to influence how they see themselves. Husbands must maintain their identity in God because giving a woman the power to determine their identity as a man will bring ruin (Proverbs 31:3). If a man allows a woman to build him up, he also allows her to tear him down.

Because women were not created to steward God's creation, they cannot truly understand that responsibility. A woman speaks from the identity and perspective of a helper, yet Genesis 3:16 tells us a wife will have different desires from her husband. A spiritually immature wife will challenge her husband's marital authority. For example, immature helpers are skilled at identifying problems but struggle to offer effective solutions. This can feel like constant complaining, making a husband feel like whatever he does is not good enough.

Men who seek to dominate spiritually immature women do so out of the fear of allowing them to influence their identity. Men who allow spiritually immature women to speak into their identity as husbands will likely abdicate their leadership responsibility because they feel their efforts are unappreciated, but God sees your efforts and will reward you accordingly. See Psalm 62:12, Proverbs 24:12, Isaiah 3:10-11, Jeremiah 17:10, Matthew 16:27, Romans 2:6, and Revelation 22:12-15.

Becoming one with a woman will influence a man's identity. We should always seek God's advice when dealing with the landmines of a marital union. As a husband, pray for the Holy Spirit to help you love your wife unconditionally and to lead her effectively. Remember that your woman was designed to be your helper. She will have more peace in her life when she can fulfill that role. Choose to be a loving husband and effective leader who maintains his identity in God. A husband who gives his wife good reasons to continue choosing him as her man gets what most men want from marriage: a wife who wants sexual intimacy with her husband.

Lesson Application

Write down at least one way you can be a better husband to your wife or future wife.

Write down an achievable and quantifiable goal that encourages you to make that improvement. What reliable and valid metric can you use to measure your improvement as a husband? (For definitions of reliable and valid, see the "Common Understanding" section in Lesson 1.)

Lesson 22

Unconditional Love

Context

Our last lesson explored the wife and stated that to be good husbands, we must love our wives unconditionally, just as Christ loved the Church (Ephesians 5:2 & Romans 5:8). This lesson builds upon and expands the previous lesson to improve our understanding of unconditional love.

What is Unconditional Love?

Unconditional love is something most people do not fully understand. Our society uses the idea of love in so many ways that its meaning is nebulous, and it has lost its definition. For example, we use the phrase "we made love" as a pleasant way to describe sex. We say "I love you" to people we secretly dislike and would never lift a finger to help. Couples get divorced because they "fell out of love."

All three of those examples show how the word has been misused. Contrary to popular opinion, love is not a feeling. Love is a choice and an action.

Love has many meanings in our culture and society, and most of them mischaracterize the true meaning. In the Greek language, love is divided into four words. "Philia" is the first word, and it describes the type of love found in strong friendships. The second word the Greeks used is "eros," which describes a romantic type of affection. It is akin to being in love with a particular person. "Storge" is the love found in family relationships. It involves empathy and affection, as well as compassion. The fourth word, "agape," describes selfless, unconditional love.

The Greek word agape is the translation on which this lesson will focus. To fully become the man God created, you must understand what agape, or unconditional love, means. We bring up the Greek word because it is the written language of the twenty-seven New Testament books.

The Greek word used in what is likely the Bible's most popular verse, John 3:16, is *agape*. Here is the verse, "For God so loved the world, that he gave his only Son, that whoever believes in him should not perish but have eternal life." Now that we know the Greek word for love in John 3:16 is a form of *agape*, we can understand that God's love for the world is selfless and unconditional.

Unconditional means without measurable conditions. To give unconditional love means to love someone simply because they exist. God's unconditional love is not based on color, ethnicity, culture, sex, sexual orientation, socio-economic status, or any other method by which we categorize people. God loves each person without preexisting conditions because each of us bears His image. We represent His glory in His creation.

The Father's Unconditional Love Example

Let's take John 3:16 a step further. God loved the image-bearers in this world He created so unconditionally that He sent Jesus to offer all of us the opportunity to have eternal life. Jesus, the son of God and a member of the Holy Trinity, a deity with all of God's attributes, accepted the penalty for all of the sins committed by all of the people who will ever exist—He took on the world's sin. Sin is what separates any person from Holy God. Christ's acceptance of sin's penalties allows every person the opportunity to maintain a connection with God, thus having eternal life.

Jesus accepted the penalty of God's wrath on our behalf even though we have done nothing to deserve it. Romans 5:8 states, "But God shows his love for us in that while we were still sinners, Christ died for us." Like John 3:16, the Greek word for love in Romans 5:8 is agape; thus, God the Father loved the people of this world so unconditionally that He allowed His beloved Son, Jesus, to take the blame for our sins. God the Father sending His Son to die for the sins of the world is perhaps the greatest example of unconditional love.

Conclusions on God's Unconditional Love

Now that we have an understanding of God's unconditional love for us, we can draw a few conclusions about the Father. First, His unconditional love for us shows that His desire for an eternal relationship with us was and is of the highest importance. After all, He sent His only beloved Son to pay the price of death on the cross for our sins.

His unconditional love also shows that we were designed to have a relationship with the one who created us. God created mankind—men and women—to extend the unconditional love within the Trinity of the Father, Son, and Holy Spirit. Our role in this world is to accept God's unconditional love and then extend that love to the other created beings God has placed in our lives.

Biblically, we know this by Jesus's response to a lawyer asking Him what the greatest commandment was. As stated earlier, in Matthew 22:37-40, Jesus responded to the lawyer's question by stating, "You shall love the LORD your God with all your heart and with all your soul and with all your mind. This is the great and first commandment. And a second is like it: You shall love your neighbor as yourself. On these two commandments depend all the Law and the Prophets." So, according to Jesus, the entire Old Testament shows that our primary role is to return God's love completely and to love the people in our lives. Again, the Greek word for both uses of love in the Great Commandment verses is agape.

Jesus's Unconditional Love Example

Jesus provides another example of unconditional love which rivals the Father's example. Jesus, the Son, dying for our sins because the Father told Him to die for our sins, is the other example of unconditional love. Romans 5:19 tells us, "For as by the one man's disobedience the many were made sinners, so by the one man's obedience the many will be made righteous." The verse demonstrates that Jesus's obedience to God provides us with the opportunity for righteousness and eternal life.

Another Bible verse tells us that obedience to God is accomplished out of love for God. In John 14:15, Jesus tells His disciples, "If you love me, you will keep my commandments." And yes, the love in this passage is the same Greek form of *agape* found in John 3:16, Romans 5:8, and Matthew 22:37 & 39; it is unconditional love. It appears that keeping the commandments or obeying God is an act of love; thus, it would be accurate to state that Jesus's obedient act of dying for the sins of the world was accomplished because He unconditionally loved the Father. In His perfection, Jesus was able to fulfill the Great Commandment He stated in Matthew 22:37 to "love the Lord your God with all your heart and with all your soul and with all your mind."

Give Unconditional Love to Others

Romans 5:8 tells us that God unconditionally loves us even though we are undeserving sinners. First John 4:19 emphasizes that God's love for us should prompt us to love Him back. We display our love through obedience to His will, which includes showing love to the other image-bearers in our lives.

To the people closest to us, such as our wives, choose to love them unconditionally at all times. Offer them unconditional love even when they have wronged us. After all, Father God and Son Jesus chose and provided unconditional love to save us from ourselves. We did not deserve their unconditional love, and we can never repay them for what they did for us.

Shouldn't we be willing to offer the same level of unconditional love to those God has placed in our care? Don't the image-bearers He has placed in our small portion of His creation—such as our wives—warrant our unconditional love? Men, when we choose to offer unconditional love to our wives, our marriages have the chance to be what they are supposed to be. Because God charged man with tending, caring for, and keeping or protecting His creation, it is our responsibility to offer unconditional love regardless of whether our wives ever offer the same love back.

Personal Experience

Once I obediently began offering unconditional love to my wife, our marriage noticeably improved. For years, I have continued to choose unconditional love out of obedience to God. The payoff of my obedience is a wife who has become a more Godly woman. My offering of unconditional love influences her to be more obedient to God because she, as the helper, witnesses the leader's obedience. We have become the best friends, confidants, and lovers that marriages are intended to be. God has rewarded my obedient efforts with a loving, Godly wife. Additionally, the love my wife and I share offers a glimpse of the love that binds the Holy Trinity.

Men, if you don't have unconditional love for your wife, ask God to give you the ability to love your woman the way He wants you to love her. If your wife is a believer in Jesus, she is also a daughter of the Father, a sister to Jesus, and a vessel of the same Holy Spirit that resides in your heart. Ask God to give you the conviction and wisdom to love His daughter the way He wants you to love her. Be the man God intended you to be and show unconditional love to the person closest to you, the woman God gave to you to tend, care for, keep, and protect. As you practice showing unconditional love to your wife, you will improve your ability to demonstrate the agape love that Jesus commands in Matthew 22:39 to the other image-bearers in your relationship circle.

Lesson Application

Your prayer life is the single most important tool you have for becoming more like our Lord Jesus Christ. During your daily prayers, ask God to help you love your wife unconditionally, change your heart, and help you see her as He sees her. Ask Him to help you become the solid, secure, and confident man God created you to be.

For this lesson, remind yourself of what unconditional love looks like by writing down one example of how you have demonstrated unconditional love to your wife in the past. If you are unmarried, write down one example of how you showed unconditional love to someone else in the past.

Lesson 23

The Family

Context

Our last lesson discussed unconditional love as a characteristic of obedience that all stewards of God's creation should possess. Our first priority as obedient, warrior-minded stewards is to unconditionally love God. The lesson ended with a focus on showing agape love to our second relational priority—our wives. This lesson builds upon the foundation of relational priorities for demonstrating *agape* love with a discussion on the family.

Establishing Priorities

As a reminder, our eternal identity is as sons of God, brothers to Jesus, and vessels of the Holy Spirit. God has tasked us with temporarily stewarding a portion of His creation that has been a war zone since the fall of man in the Garden of Eden. War produces chaos, and we must have a warrior-minded focus to ensure we spend our limited resources, particularly time, wisely. Prioritizing tasks is how we limit confusion caused by the spiritual warfare into which we are born.

Our first priority is to care for and protect God's image-bearers. Jesus stated this very thing when He provided the Great Commandments in Matthew 22:37-40. Our Lord commands us to love

God with all of our heart, soul, and mind. Choosing to love God makes our relationship with Him our most important priority.

The second commandment our Lord gave was to love your neighbor as yourself. Loving your neighbor is not the same as assuming responsibility for what God has placed in your care. Yes, we should demonstrate love to all people by choosing the best action for them. But God placed some people directly within our sphere of influence. We call these people family.

The Family's Priority

As stated in the previous lesson, a wife is a man's second-most important relationship. She is the image-bearer God has provided to His steward to help tend and keep His creation. As the weaker vessel, being the more fragile half of the union, a wife needs to know her husband has her back at all times so she can bring her talents to the table. As a natural nurturer, a wife is often the glue that binds a family. She will sacrifice herself out of love for her family, but she must trust that her strong man can carry the load that she cannot or that she drops. Further, she needs to know that her husband is a warrior who will always seek to protect her and will sacrifice himself for her if need be.

Because she is a mature believer, my wife submits to my leadership over our family; however, she is a daughter of the Most High God, and her primary relationship is with our shared heavenly Father. While our relationship is never perfect, I always try to remember she is my Creator's daughter, a sister to my Lord and Savior Jesus, and a vessel of the same Holy Spirit that resides in my heart. As her husband my job is to show her the love that Christ has shown me.

For those of us with a woman, the third-most important relationship is the children a marital union produces. Like our women, the image-bearing children God places in our care need to know they are safe and unconditionally loved by their family's leader. A child's first understanding of God is through the family's father. Of course, a good earthly father who loves his children wants them to accept Jesus as Lord and Savior. More importantly, God wants them to accept Jesus as Lord and Savior, and He expects earthly fathers to guide their children to Jesus. Earthly fathers should model what Jesus has done and continues doing in their lives to influence their children's decisions.

For men who do not have a wife but have children, the children move up to priority number two in relationships. Regardless of the circumstances of a wife-less fatherhood, such as divorce, God created the child or children out of the man's seed. A child will always look to his/her mother and father for the unconditional love all image-bearers need; thus, a man with children but no wife must prayerfully seek ways to be a Godly influence on his children.

Men, whether you are married, divorced, never-married, or widowed, don't ever disparage a child's mother. A mother's womb is where all identity begins. Do not tell a child that he or she came into this world from a bad place. Jeremiah 17:10 and Hebrews 4:13 tell us that God sees what we do and knows why we do it. Do not slander your children's mother. Always take the high road when talking to a child about his/her mother. James 4:11-12 tells us God is the only one holy enough to judge. Children eventually become adults and will see their parents' flaws for themselves.

For men who are not yet married and have no children, the relationship with family is the second most important priority. This could be parents and siblings. This could be non-blood image-bearers such as friends. After a man's relationship with God, the people closest to the man need to see Jesus living through him.

The image-bearers we have stewardship responsibilities over—our women and children—require food, shelter, and clothing. They recognize our God-given leadership and expect us to provide them with these necessities. More importantly, God expects us to provide them with these necessities. First Timothy 5:8 states, "But if anyone does not provide for his relatives, and especially for members of his household, he has denied the faith and is worse than an unbeliever." God created us to work and keep His creation. We should not shirk that responsibility. Further, our vocation must meet the needs of our women and children. Being a starving artist is not a valid option when other image-bearers rely on you for their well-being. Our priorities of time and effort expenditures are God, then our wives, then our children, and then the work that sustains those relationships.

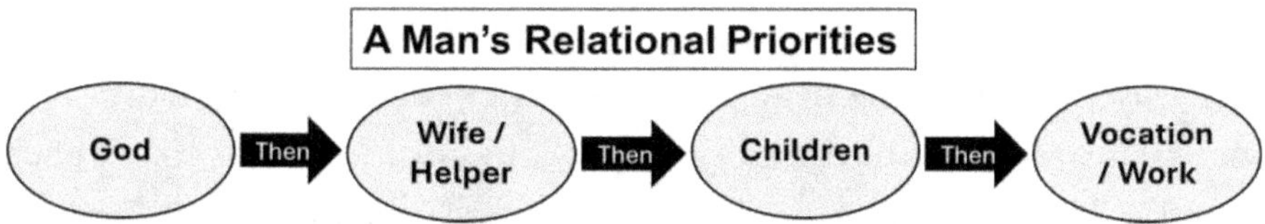

Figure 7 - A Man's Relational Priorities

For unmarried and childless men, a vocation that supports others is not as important since they only have themselves to support; however, those men should make life decisions that will allow them to support a future family. No matter our career decisions, what we do is less important than who we provide for. As men our stewardship priority is to ensure the image-bearers in our sphere of control are healthy, protected, and loved.

Earthly vs. Eternal Father

I will share some personal stories to reinforce how we must prioritize the image-bearers God places in our care. Right now, I steward a peaceful family, but I know what it's like to be the steward of a family in chaos. One of the reasons for the Discipled Warriors Ministry is to provide all men with the truth they need to have peace in their families. Some men will relate to my personal family stories, and all men can learn from my stories to improve their families.

The first story occurred when God spoke to me and emphasized a vital truth about family. The story begins a month after our youngest daughter's thirteenth birthday. Her appendix ruptured. At that time, she was making numerous poor decisions, so when she stated that her stomach hurt, my wife and I thought she was trying to get out of attending school. She complained about her stomach for five days before we finally brought her to a nearby emergency room. From there, she was transported to our regional children's hospital and had her first major surgery the following morning when her appendix was removed. Because of the damage caused to her abdominal contents, more surgeries were needed.

Two days later, the dead portions of her small and large intestines were removed, and the live portions of her intestines were stapled back together. She was placed in the intensive care unit with her abdominal wall left open to ensure the intestinal staples held and there was adequate blood flow. Two days following that surgery, her third significant surgery occurred, which was to close her abdomen and allow her intestines to restart. The doctors stated the third surgery was going to be the most complicated.

I was driving to the hospital the morning of our daughter's third surgery, and I used the time to pray. God spoke to me at a stoplight near the hospital. At the stoplight, I asked God to protect my daughter. He responded to my request by saying, "Whose daughter?"

I don't remember the remainder of our conversation, but His question/statement left me in a peaceful state. God gave me peace at perhaps my scariest moment as our family's steward. When I arrived at the hospital, I was able to pass along my peaceful state to my wife, our other children, and our extended family. Our daughter's third surgery went well, and today, she has minimal complications from the life-threatening surgeries she experienced over a five-day period.

God gave me peace when I needed it most. More important, He gave me a truth that jump-started this ministry. The truth is that I am an earthly father. I temporarily steward the children God places in my care. As their temporary steward, I have the essential task of ensuring they are introduced to the only one who offers eternal life, the Lord Jesus Christ. My earthly children belong to their Creator who loves and cares for them more deeply than I can ever understand and wants them to choose Him as their eternal Father.

They Have Choice

An important job we have as earthly fathers and temporary stewards is to ensure our children become responsible, independent adults. During our time as earthly fathers, we must give our children every opportunity to accept Jesus as their Lord and Savior. If they accept Jesus, they become an eternal member of the Creator's family. We can do everything in our power to show them the right choice, but we cannot make that choice for them.

As image-bearers, our wives and children have the same level of choice that we do. They might choose poorly. They might choose paths of destruction. When they do, it will break our hearts because we love and want what is best for them.

This must be how God feels when we break His heart. As leaders of families, we get an idea of how He loves us and desires us to make good choices. Remember that no matter our sins, God continues to show us love, patience, kindness, and generosity. Extend what the Eternal Father shows you to your family members.

Speaking Identity Into Grandchildren

Some of us live long enough to become grandfathers. Our time as God's representative to a child transitions to a different role. My next personal story emphasizes that our role as grandfathers might be our most potent influence.

I was born to an alcoholic dad and a schizophrenic mother. As you may guess, my childhood home was dysfunctional. My earthly father was not the example I had of a Godly man. Thankfully, I had a paternal grandfather who provided that example.

I was able to spend nearly every holiday at his home and multiple weeks each summer with him. My family moved a lot, so my grandfather's house felt like home to me. I felt safe there, allowing my grandfather to speak manhood identity into me. When I was with him, we did something every day. We would work in his yard or his farm, visit other people in their homes, have lunch in diners, and visit with others there. Whatever we did, he always allowed me to have my own opinions and work through my issues. I cannot remember him speaking down to me or treating my ideas like they had no merit. He offered the one thing all men need: respect.

As I transitioned into young adulthood, I strayed from God's path. I knew what was right, but I chose what was wrong. Toward the end of my "wild, young adult phase," my grandfather died. At his funeral, I remember thinking that if I could lead a life like he did, my life in this world would be a good one.

After his funeral, I began seeking a sincere relationship with God. Because I started seeking God, I have accomplished things He created me to do. In return, He has given me the desires of my heart. God has given me a good family and a good home. I am secure in who I am and routinely experience peace, hope, and joy. See Psalm 37:4 and Matthew 6:21 for explanations of how our hearts and God's gifts are intricately tied. While I learned from everyone around me, my grandfather was the earthly example of what it means to be a respected man. I praise God for blessing me with his example and influence on my life.

Childhood Trauma Influences Adult Decisions

I was blessed to have a Godly man to model my life after, but abundant research shows our personalities are established around age five. This means that whatever we experience before the age of five, the good and bad significantly shape how we perceive and interact with people—trust or mistrust in others; secure, confident, and independent; or anxious, self-doubt, and fearful. Early childhood trauma can be a root cause of poor decisions for adults.

Again, my parents' home was dysfunctional and chaotic, and the traumatic events I had at an early age negatively played into my decisions as an adult. I recognized my parents' flaws when I was about thirteen and decided I would not follow in their footsteps. As stated earlier, I was immature as a young man and made numerous poor decisions.

One of the poor choices I made as a young adult was to get married at the age of twenty. I wasn't ready for marriage, but because of my pride, I thought I was. Additionally, I selected a wife who had similar mental instabilities as my mother. To make matters worse, I prioritized my professional life over my personal life and forced my flawed wife to care for our home, which was a task that she was incapable of handling.

To use a term borrowed from 2 Corinthians 6:14, we were unequally yoked. Further, I did not seek God's guidance in selecting a wife. I was a young, talented, and driven man who chose marriage out of lust. I lacked the patience, kindness, and forgiveness a wife needs from her husband. My first wife paid the price for my immaturity and pride.

Thankfully, God protected me from many of my bad choices. He saved me from my decisions, but He did not save my first marriage. After eight years of holding on, trying to make our marriage and family work, God told me to get divorced, or I would die. I filed for divorce and got full custody of the two children my wife and I had together.

While my first wife professed a Christian faith, her actions did not demonstrate that faith. Additionally, I did not offer her a home where her husband loved her unconditionally. Instead, I was demanding and uncompromising. Had I demonstrated the unconditional love God calls His stewards to possess and pass on, she may have chosen faith and sought a peaceful relationship with God. Regardless, to my knowledge, she still has not accepted Jesus as Lord and Savior.

God forgave me for the divorce, allowing my current marriage to thrive. Unfortunately, I passed on to my children what I experienced: divorced parents and a dysfunctional home. I can't change my past failures, and I cannot deny that I caused harm to others. I absolutely contributed to our broken family.

That divorce occurred nearly three decades ago. The two children produced from that marriage are now both married and both have young children. Thankfully, both have made better spouse choices than I did and seem to have healthy families. I still pray for them and their spouses.

For my grandchildren, I am trying to be the grandfather that I had. I want my grandchildren to see patience, kindness, and forgiveness in the patriarch of their family. I want them to experience the calmness, peace, and love that a mature, Godly man can offer when they are respected for simply existing within my sphere of influence.

Lesson Application - Choosing to love God as your top priority is the key to maintaining focus on the spiritual warfare battlefield. Write down what you can do to continually encourage yourself to choose a loving relationship with God. What habits can you develop, and how do those habits specifically apply to your needs?

Lesson 24

Childhood Wounds

Context

The previous lesson briefly discussed how childhood wounds can negatively influence adult choices. Here's what happens: When a child is physically or emotionally wounded, innocence is taken and replaced with the knowledge that the world can be dangerous. Because the world is dangerous, early wounds are necessary to begin directing decisions in a child's life.

Childhood wounds—particularly traumatic ones—can produce irrational fear that dominates a lifetime of decision-making. Fear-based decisions severely limit a person's ability to choose good paths. Fear impedes a person's ability to trust others or take reasonable risks. When heeded long enough, fear-based decisions become the person's identity. People whose identity is marked by fear have a difficult time trusting in the goodness of God and will avoid taking the risk of accepting Jesus as Lord and Savior. Believers who continue making fear-based decisions live a lesser life than God intended.

Ephesians 6:12 tells us our fight in this world is against "..the spiritual forces of evil." Wounding children is a common way our enemy causes God's image-bearers to make fear-based decisions as adults. John 8:44 tells us the enemy is a liar, and his lies about our identity are meant to keep us in fear. Second Timothy 1:7 states that God did not create us to live in fear; He created us to be extensions of His power.

Now, all of us have spiritual warfare wounds. Most of us have childhood wounds that have not healed, causing us to make poor adult decisions. The expression "hurt people, hurt people" is popular because this world has many wounded image-bearers whose decision-making begins with fear and self-preservation. Healing our past wounds removes the lies we hold onto that keep us in fear. Removing a fear-induced identity allows us to break whatever cycle of hurt in which we may be stuck.

Lesson 16 covered how we remove strongholds the enemy has established because of our sin. As a reminder, our enemy establishes strongholds to prevent us from sharing the Gospel message in word or deed. Strongholds are established because of our sins as well as the damage we incur from the sins of other image-bearers. This lesson will discuss how to remove strongholds caused by past wounds. To explain how strongholds get established from the wounds of another person's sin, I will offer a personal example.

Personal Example

The year before I entered kindergarten, my parents, my younger sister, and I lived in a double-story apartment complex that surrounded a large playground on at least three sides. In that complex, I witnessed a sexual assault at the age of four.

On the day of the assault, a few of us smaller kids who were in the playground went into the apartment of one of the kids with whom we were playing. I'm not sure why we went into his downstairs apartment, but I remember the kid our age had an older, teenage brother. The teenage brother called us into a room and proceeded to sexually accost one of the smaller kids with whom I went into the apartment.

Now, I don't remember everything, so I will list what I do and don't remember. I remember the sexual assault occurred on a bunk bed. I cannot remember if I was outside of the room when the attack started or if I left the room once the assault began. I remember being scared and thinking I had to get out of the apartment as soon as possible. I remember leaving while the assault was being carried out, as I could hear screaming as I left, and I remember feeling bad for not helping the kid who was being assaulted by the older brother. I do not remember what happened to the other kids who went into the apartment with me. I remember running home to my family's apartment, which was diagonally across the playground.

I do not remember talking to my parents about the assault. I'm not sure why I didn't talk to them, but I do remember feeling shame for being a witness to something I knew was wrong. I remember not wanting to play with the kid who had the rapist for a teenage brother, and I declined to go into other people's homes by myself for years following the incident.

Wounding Effects

In reliving the memory of the incident, I know that I felt fear for my personal safety and shame for not helping the accosted child. I began to wonder why my parents never warned me that something like that could happen. I began feeling that my parents could not or would not fully protect me. I remember feeling that I could not trust them to tell me the whole truth and that I would have to be careful to protect myself, even though I knew my parents would never have placed me into a situation they thought might cause me harm.

I also remember thinking they were unable to prevent me from harm, so I had to be responsible for my safety. The realization that my parents could not protect me added to my fear, establishing a stronghold that caused me to be overly cautious and distrustful of the intentions of others. That childhood wound likely contributes to my difficulty establishing close friendships.

Another effect of the stronghold was a profound desire to be strong enough never to become a victim of someone else's sins; thus, the incident likely played a positive role in the paths I chose later in life. For example, I became a punishing linebacker in football for the remainder of my youth. As a young adult, I chose a military profession where I became a highly trained combat soldier. Romans 8:28 tells us that "in all things God works for the good of those who love him, who have been called according to his purpose." My fear of becoming a victim allowed God to use my childhood wound to influence me to become strong, durable, and self-sufficient.

While my desire to avoid victimhood was good, it caused other problems beyond a distrust of others. As a young and immature adult male, I lacked understanding, kindness, and forgiveness for people who were victims. Many times, I have felt like those who were suffering brought their dilemma upon themselves. Not surprisingly, God has used my lack of sympathy for others as part of my sanctification process. He has placed me in situations where I was the only person who could care for someone's needs, and I was grudgingly obedient to what was clearly His will. I still struggle with sympathy, but I recognize that choosing compassion for others in obedience to His will is something I must continue doing to receive the blessings He pours out of the sanctification process.

Shame was the other impact of the sexual assault I witnessed. I felt shame for not helping the boy, but the incident opened the door to another form of shame. While I knew the incident was wrong, I wondered why the teenage brother sexually attacked the young boy. The exposure to fleshly lust at an unprepared age forced questions for which I had no answers. Further, the act was an intentional aggravated sexual assault, which dehumanized an image-bearer. I was forced to think through some of humanity's darkest sins before I was adequately prepared to understand what happened, causing a curiosity about sex that produced more shame in my adolescence. Thankfully, because I am God's child, He has cleansed me from sexual shame and transformed my mind into knowing that my marriage is His gift that allows me to express sexual desires sinlessly.

Writing About a Wound

I have written down the childhood wound incident I shared. Like the Removing Strongholds exercise from lesson 16, you will write down the specific details you remember about an incident that wounded you when you were a child, preferably the earliest wound you can remember. Remembering and reliving moments in our lives that caused us pain is difficult, but let me explain the importance of doing so.

Writing the specifics about the incident allowed me to think through some of the details I may have missed had I only talked about the incident. Writing down the details forced me to grapple with the incident and accept what had happened. Taking the time to write about the incident also allowed me to understand my life's path better.

Ultimately, we must know what problems exist before we can fix those problems. Because our past wounds likely influence our current decisions, particularly poor ones, understanding what happened in the past is vital to healing a present wound. So, take time to write down as many details as you can remember about the earliest childhood wound you received.

A way to list out the details is to use the five Ws and one H method discussed in Lesson 15. That method begins by listing out the words who, what, when, where, why, and how, and then providing as many details as possible that correspond to each one-word question. The five Ws and one H method is not the only way. For example, I began by writing down what I remembered and then described how the incident influenced my life afterward, in writing.

Jesus Heals Wounds

Once you have written down everything you can remember about the wound, it's time to ask Jesus for healing. Jesus can heal all of our wounds. Along with eternal salvation, He is in the business of healing. Jeremiah 17:14 states, "Heal me, O Lord, and I shall be healed; save me, and I shall be saved, for you are my praise." Psalm 147:3 states that the Lord "heals the brokenhearted / and binds up their wounds." Matthew 9:35 states, "Jesus went throughout all the cities and villages, teaching in their synagogues and proclaiming the gospel of the kingdom and healing every disease and every affliction."

Three of the gospels discuss the story of Jesus healing Peter's mother-in-law in Capernaum and what He did after He healed her. In Matthew 8:16, we are told that Jesus "cast out the spirits with a word and healed all who were sick." In Mark 1:34, we are told that Jesus "healed many who were sick with various diseases." In Luke 4:40, we are told that Jesus "laid his hands on every one [who was sick with various diseases] and healed them."

A fact we do not often hear is that because Yahweh created time, He is not bound by time as we are. Jesus can heal old wounds. Further, He was there when you incurred the wound. Numerous verses support this claim. Proverbs 15:3, Job 34:21-22, and Hebrews 4:13 tell us that God sees everything we do. And, since He is the breath of life, according to Genesis 7:22 and Job 33:4, He is the very air we breathe. Jesus knows what happened to you and why it happened. He wants to heal you and is waiting for you to ask Him.

Lesson Application - The Healing Prayer

When you're ready, find a private setting and establish temporary authority over the space by saying out loud, "In the name, power, and authority of Jesus, I command all voices to be silent except for the Father, the Son, or the Holy Spirit." Again, God can read our thoughts, but evil spirits cannot.

After establishing authority, share the details about the childhood wound you wrote down. You can speak them out loud or silently. Don't hold back on the details. Use your notes if you need to.

Remember, prayer is a conversation between you and our Creator. So, while you pray, be attentive to His presence, guidance, and wisdom. He created you to be a warrior-minded steward for His Kingdom and wants to free you of the strongholds incurred from past wounds.

Once you've shared the details of your wound, ask Jesus to heal you from the wounds you received. Ask Him to help you forgive the person or people responsible for your wound. Then, ask Him to forgive the person or people who wounded you.

Write down pertinent details of what you experienced during your healing prayer.

Do not read until you have written down details about your healing prayer.

As you relived the memories in your prayer, you may have seen Jesus in the memories. Don't be overly surprised if you did, as I saw Him when I conducted my healing prayer. I saw Him guiding me out of the apartment in a protective manner. He was beside me, backing me away from the room where the attack was occurring. Protectively, His hand was on my chest while He faced the room where the assault took place. His face held a disappointed, stern look.

I also saw that He was kneeling next to the boy who was being sexually assaulted. He was holding the boy's hand, looking at his face simultaneously with sadness and love. In my memory, I wasn't shocked to see Jesus in two places during the same event. After all, He is the Almighty God.

By showing me that He was protecting me from harm, He reaffirmed a deep-seated belief I've always had that He has always been with me. By letting me see Him holding the hand of the boy who was attacked, Jesus let me know that He is with others even in their darkest moments. I don't fully understand how, but seeing Jesus next to the other boy also let me know the other boy overcame the assault he endured; thus, I no longer feel shame for not helping the boy because Jesus was there with him and helped him heal from his wound.

Lesson 25

Vocation

Context

In the previous lesson, we asked Jesus to heal our childhood wounds so we can fully become the Kingdom warriors God created us to be. Asking Jesus to heal past wounds helps to cleanse our hearts. A clean heart is necessary for sanctification, which is the process of learning to act on what God's Spirit reveals.

Responsibility Revisited

Past lessons have demonstrated that God's task for men is the stewardship of a portion of His creation. A good steward prioritizes the care and protection of the image-bearers God places in his portion of creation. Generally, this means decisions must seek the highest good for the steward's wife and then his children. Because this world is a warzone, a steward's next priority is providing the means for the nourishment and safety of his family. A man works a job in exchange for those means.

Generally, we think of our jobs as necessary evils. If we're lucky, we might have a career or profession where the necessity of work encourages spiritual growth and maturity. Whatever we do to accumulate the means to support ourselves and those we are responsible for, we should think of that work effort as a vocation, not just a job.

Vocation > Job

This lesson uses the word vocation as the representative synonym for the definition encompassing job, work, profession, calling, etc. Colossians 3:23-24 tells us that whatever we do, we're "serving the Lord." We serve Christ when we ensure that image-bearers have their needs met, and the word "vocation" aptly describes these efforts, as it implies suitability and dedication.

Vocation includes Jesus's commands in Matthew 28:19 and Mark 16:15 to "make disciples of all nations" and spread "the gospel to the whole creation." Not all of us are called to have a religious vocation, but we are all commanded to share the Gospel message and make disciples. We do this first in our homes, then with others in our circle of influence.

Vocation is how we contribute to God's creation while ensuring that our people receive the benefits of our efforts. Questions to ask ourselves include: What are we doing to improve the world God created? And how can we ensure the image bearers who rely on us have what they need to thrive while gaining ground for God's Kingdom?

When responding to those questions, it is essential to remember that our vocation is not our identity. For those who have accepted Jesus, our most authentic identity is as sons of the Father, brothers to Jesus, and vessels of the Holy Spirit.

Identity Revisited

Our vocation stems from our identity as believers who are reborn in Christ (See Romans 6:4; 2 Corinthians 5:17; and Colossians 3:10). We belong to the Body of Christ, which metaphorically describes how all of us are needed to form a complete and healthy Body (See Romans 12:5, 1 Corinthians 10:17 and 12:27, Ephesians 4:12, and Colossians

1:24). Members of the Body of Christ possess diverse gifts suited to particular functions.

First Corinthians 12:12 states, "The body is a unit, though it is made up of many parts; and though all its parts are many, they form one Body. So it is with Christ." God created us to minister to the Body of Christ in different ways for different purposes. All of us were designed to perform a needed function within the Body.

"The Lord God took the man and put him in the garden in Eden to work it and keep it" because it was good for the man to have responsibility (Genesis 2:15). Similar to the responsibility of marriage and raising children, we are better men when we have to accomplish specific tasks. Additionally, when others rely on us to complete specific tasks, we are more likely to accomplish them and serve others in the process. Serving others keeps us from sinning because sin stems from selfish desires.

Strive for Excellence

Because we are vessels of the Holy Spirit, we have no excuse for mediocrity. We should be excellent in what we do. We should be dependable in showing up on time and working until the task is accomplished. We should have a good attitude and not look to disparage others. People we work with should see that we are better than the median, the standard, or what is normal, allowing us the opportunity and platform to share the Gospel and make disciples through our actions.

Because we represent Christ, we should choose a vocation that complements the talents God has given us. In Ephesians 4:1, Paul urged his audience to "...walk in a manner worthy of the calling to which you have been called." This verse applies to our vocation. God designed us to be talented in certain areas and enjoy particular tasks. We should choose vocations that fit the talents of God's design for each of us. Utilizing our God-given talents will produce an overflow of blessings to benefit those around us.

Money is necessary because it is how we conduct transactional negotiations in this world, but the fact is, we are born naked and will leave this world naked (Job 1:21). We are spiritual souls with temporary bodies. Money is physical, not spiritual. God created our souls to be in a relationship with Him; "more stuff" will not satisfy our souls. Satisfaction comes from choosing to follow His will, not from what the world says is important, which is often money. So, avoid working simply for the sake of money. The overflow of our talents comes in many forms.

Our example to follow and emulate, the Lord Jesus Christ, denied Himself for the sake of others. Philippians 2:3-7 states, "Do nothing from selfish ambition or conceit, but in humility count others more significant than yourselves. Let each of you look not only to his own interests, but also to the interests of others. Have this mind among yourselves, which is yours in Christ Jesus, who, though he was in the form of God, did not count equality with God a thing to be grasped, but emptied himself, by taking the form of a servant, being born in the likeness of men."

When we know our eternity will be to exist with our Creator in paradise, what do the trinkets of this world have to offer us? Solomon states in Ecclesiastes 12:13 that our whole duty is to "fear God and keep His commandments." In our vocation, the people we work with should see Jesus in us. Maybe our demonstration of the goodness that comes from being His disciple can encourage others also to choose Jesus.

Bible Verses About Work

Let's review some Scripture related to work. According to Job 34:21, Proverbs 5:21, Jeremiah 23:24, and Hebrews 4:13, God sees everything we do. Further, we will have to give an account to Jesus for our actions according to Matthew 25:31-32, Romans 2:16, 2 Corinthians 5:10, and Revelation 2:23. So, if God sees what we do and we have to give an account of what we have done, we should accept our stewardship responsibilities and do our best to meet and exceed man's expectations of those responsibilities.

Regardless of how challenging those responsibilities are, know that God will provide you with what you need to complete them. Scriptures supporting this claim include Romans 8:28, 2 Corinthians 9:8, and Philippians 4:19. When life becomes difficult, we should praise God because we know that these challenging times will ultimately make us stronger. See Acts 14:22, James 1:2-4, and 1 Peter 1:6-7 for scriptural passages that support praising God in difficult times.

In Matthew 22:21, Jesus told His audience to "give back to Caesar what is Caesar's." Jesus's statement lets us know that this world's system requires money. Numerous passages, including Deuteronomy 25:4, Leviticus 19:13, Luke 10:7, and 1 Timothy 5:18, speak to the need for our labor to receive financial compensation.

When we labor, we should not remain in poverty. Proverbs 13:4, 14:23, and 18:9 all state that we should work to avoid an impoverished life. New Testament passages that also state the need to avoid poverty include Galatians 6:7-9, Ephesians 4:28, and 2 Thessalonians 3:10. Poverty is a relative term because multiple measurement methods are used to determine it. For example, one person might believe he is in poverty while another person with the same income believes he lives a prosperous life.

The Good Life

A prosperous life begins with being content with what God has provided from your vocation. Scripture that discusses the attitude of contentment includes Ecclesiastes 7:14, Philippians 4:11-12, Hebrews 13:5, and 1 Timothy 6:6-10. Contentment with God's provisions allows for a peaceful and quiet life. According to Proverbs 17:1, Ecclesiastes 4:6, and 1 Thessalonians 4:11-12, a quiet life is a good life.

A good life is where you ensure the people you are charged with stewarding have what they need, and you have something left over to give to the less fortunate God places in your life. John 15:8 states, "By this my Father is glorified, that you bear much fruit and so prove to be my disciples." Acts 20:35 states, "In all things I have shown you that by working hard in this way we must help the weak and remember the words of the Lord Jesus, how he himself said, 'It is more blessed to give than to receive.'" Titus 3:14 states, "And let our people learn to devote themselves to good works, so as to help cases of urgent need, and not be unfruitful." A man who takes care of his own and helps the needy lives a good life. Regardless of income, sound finances begin with money management.

80/20 Rule

Tithing is the start to managing your finances. I became convinced of the need to tithe in my mid-thirties. When I told my wife we were going to start tithing, she was initially resistant. It was one of the few times in our marriage that I did not allow for a discussion. I told her she needed to get on board with my decision because we would tithe from that moment forward. Financially, that was the best decision I have ever made.

God has blessed my family since He convicted me to begin tithing. Additionally, my wife has seen how God has blessed us and is now a big believer in tithing. The main verse that convinced me to begin tithing is Malachi 3:10, which states, "Bring the full tithe into the storehouse, that there may be food in my house. And thereby put me to the test, says the Lord of hosts, if I will not open the windows of heaven for you and pour down for you a blessing until there is no more need."

Soon after I became convinced of my need to tithe, I began using an 80/20 rule for my earned income, and have taught this rule to my children. The rule is based on every dollar you earn. The first ten cents of that dollar goes to God as a tithe. The next ten cents go into a long-term savings account. The remaining 80 cents of the dollar is what our family lives on.

If you are looking for a simple method to manage finances, the 80/20 rule has given me a life of plenty. I'm sure there are other suitable methods to manage money. Whichever one you use, remember that it all belongs to God anyway, so start tithing to show your gratitude for His blessings. Over time, you will see how He gives you more than you can give Him.

Tithe to the local church you attend to assist the congregation in maintaining a presence in your community. Honor God by giving where you are fed. Be a source of nourishment to the garden you eat from, so you can continue to receive its bounty.

Lesson Application - Talking to God

When I wasn't sure what my work should be, a man I trust suggested I ask God what vocation He wanted me to have. My discussion with God about the work He wanted me to perform has provided *shalom*. Because of my experience, I am going to ask you to do the same thing.

Find a quiet place to talk to God and assume temporary authority over the space. Pray to the Father. Thank Him for giving you the ability to work. Thank Him for the work you have done. Ask Him to show you the vocation He wants for you.

He might tell you that you are right where He wants you. He might tell you to go in a different direction. Regardless of what God might tell you, we want to do what He designed and wants us to do. Remember, we serve Him; we don't serve ourselves. We expand His Kingdom when we do His will, not ours, and that should be our daily endeavor.

Write down any insights gained from your prayer/discussion with God about the vocation He wants for you.

Lesson 26

The Church

Context

In the last lesson, we discussed the need to seek vocations that suit God's design for each of us. Whatever work we perform, our vocations should contribute to the expansion of His Kingdom. This lesson will explore how strengthening the Church, big C, is essential to this expansion.

Relational Priorities

We'll start by reviewing a man's priorities of effort. Establishing and following priorities is important because of time constraints, finite energy, and resources. We cannot do everything, so we make choices based on levels of importance. Knowing and following priorities makes decision-making easier.

In all choices, we start with the fundamental truth that God exists. The Bible tells us who He is, that we bear His image, are responsible for managing His creation, and, by His grace, are offered an eternal existence with Him through faith in Jesus Christ. Clearly, God wants a relationship with us in this world and in heaven; thus, maintaining a close relationship with God is our top priority.

A man's second relational priority is his wife. A wife is the woman God gives to a man to help him steward his portion of creation. The woman exists and was designed to help her husband; thus, a wise husband chooses what is best for his wife when it aligns with God's will.

Children are a man's third relational priority. Children fulfill God's command in Genesis 1:28 to "be fruitful and multiply and fill the earth." Stewardship of children is temporary—while a wife is permanent; thus, a wise steward chooses what is best for his children in service of God's will and his wife's needs. Men without wives or children should be spiritually, emotionally, and financially ready to provide shelter and safety to any image bearers God may place in their lives.

A man's fourth priority is his vocation because of his relationship as the God-ordained leader of his family. The responsibility of leading a family means a man must provide the material needs of his family members. Thus, choices about meeting those needs are prioritized over other decisions as long as they fall under God's will and support the needs of his wife and children. Families experience and witness God's provisions when their leader provides for them without asking for anything in return.

This brings us to a man's fifth relational priority, the Church. As God's steward, a man prioritizes meeting the needs of his family. The Church was created to meet the needs of all image-bearers in God's creation. Because of the Church's responsibility to all people, a man should prioritize what is best for the Church over his relationships with friends, extended family, political affiliations, or hobbies.

Purpose of the Church

The Church is prioritized after a man's vocation because it is God's hands, mouth, and feet in this warzone in which we exist. According to 1 Corinthians 12:12-27, the Church is the Body of Christ, which means the Church should do the things that Jesus Christ would do if He were physically present on the earth. The Church can perform God's will because Body members have His Spirit residing in their hearts (Romans 8:9). The variety of spiritual gifts given to each Body member allows the Church to meet diverse needs (Romans 12:4-5 and Colossians 1:17-18).

Members of the Body use their gifts to expand and gain ground for God's Kingdom by opening people's eyes and turning them "from darkness to light and from the power of Satan to God" in two primary ways (Acts 26:18). The first is that we share the Gospel to bring in more Body members (Mark 16:15). The second is that we support local congregations so members of the Body are spiritually discipled into mature Christians who can be warriors for God (Matthew 28:19).

The Church is represented by local congregations that have numerous purposes. A primary purpose, according to Ephesians 4:14, is to teach believers biblical truths "so that we may no longer be children, tossed to and fro by the waves and carried about by every wind of doctrine, by human cunning, by craftiness in deceitful schemes." In addition to ministry leaders teaching biblical truths, local congregations allow believers to "instruct one another" in the gospel message (Romans 15:14), fulfilling the Proverbs 27:17 maxim of iron sharpening iron.

A local church also provides the space for believers to worship corporately. It is where we can address "...one another in psalms and hymns and spiritual songs, singing and making melody to the Lord with your heart, giving thanks always and for everything to God the Father in the name of our Lord Jesus Christ" (Ephesians 5:19-20). It is a place of fellowship where, according to Hebrews 10:24-25, Christians can "...stir up one another to love and good works, not neglecting to meet together, as is the habit of some, but encouraging one another." Romans 12:10 and Ephesians 4:32 tell us that a local church encourages kindness, compassion, and loving others.

A local church is where believers can gather to observe the Lord's Supper, Communion, or Eucharist as commanded in 1 Corinthians 11:23-26. A local church promotes, teaches, and practices the act of prayer, fulfilling the command in Philippians 4:6-7 to "not be anxious about anything, but in everything, by prayer and petition, with thanksgiving, present your requests to God. And the peace of God, which transcends all understanding, will guard your hearts and your minds in Christ Jesus." A local church is where new believers can be baptized, an action commanded by Matthew 28:19 and Mark 16:15. Finally, local congregations should "look after [the] orphans and widows" in their area, as called for in James 1:27.

Supporting the Church

Thus, we support the big C *Church* when we support a local congregation. Supporting the Body of Christ in this world is vital to expanding the Kingdom of Heaven. Support can come in many forms. What's important is to bloom where you are planted. In other words, if you see a need that you can meet, you are likely witnessing a God-given opportunity to serve the Body. When confronted with a need you can meet, obediently meet it without complaint or expectation of adulation. Demonstrate and deepen your faith through quietly serving the Lord and giving glory to Him whenever the opportunity arises.

As you meet the needs God places before you, know that He will often move you in a direction in which you don't know what the end result will be. When you're in that position, don't be anxious. As Philippians 4:6-7 states, express your concerns and worries to God so that He can give you supernatural peace. Then, begin moving in the direction He points out, relying on the promise of Proverbs 3:5-6, which tells us to "Trust in the Lord with all your heart, and do not lean on your own understanding. In all your ways acknowledge him, and he will make straight your paths."

As you work through the complications of any new endeavor, you will learn about yourself and gain a better understanding of our God. Sometimes, the new endeavor doesn't work out, but that doesn't mean it was time wasted. Anytime you gain a better appreciation of how you fit into God's plan, you are deepening your faith in the Lord. Hebrews 11:6 states that "without faith it is impossible to please him, for whoever would draw near to God must believe that he exists and that he rewards those who seek him." Second Corinthians 5:7 reminds us that "we walk by faith, not by sight."

Sometimes the new endeavor God points you to works out better than you could have ever hoped. When that happens, be sure to glorify the God who blessed you with the means to complete the task He set before you. In John 15:8, Jesus told His disciples that "His Father" was glorified when they produced much fruit. First Corinthians 10:31 tells us to do everything "to the glory of God."

The development of the Discipled Warriors Ministry was started by God showing me a need I could meet. Once I understood the need He showed me and had a semi-clear idea of the direction He was sending me, I asked a wise and educated man to be my sounding board so the ministry's teachings had a firm theological footing. I could not have presented the ministry's teachings without his assurance and encouragement that the ministry's message was important for men to hear.

I provide my story to demonstrate that we often must rely on other Body members to accomplish the tasks God places before us. In relying on others, we strengthen the Church through unified goals. Additionally, asking a brother or sister for help allows them to express their God-given talents. God designed us to assist one another, so our seeking support could very well be a blessing to the person from whom we ask for help.

Securing the Kingdom

While developing the Discipled Warriors Ministry was an act of obedience in meeting a need God had shown me, I am personally motivated in the ministry's success to secure my family. I want my children and grandchildren to live in a society where strong men—who faithfully follow our Lord Jesus Christ—make it their business to clear out evil whenever and wherever they see it. For too long, men in our society have abdicated the responsibility of caring for God's creation.

Many men spend their energies on the pursuit of hedonistic pleasures, leaving behind a wake of fragile image-bearers who need protection from the evils of this world. Instead of accepting the stewardship role God has blessed them with and flourishing in that role, many men have pawned their God-ordained responsibilities to women. God did not create women to lead families. When men abdicate their stewardship role, the Church withers, and everyone suffers from an unchecked and insidious evil that consumes society like malignant cancer.

The eighteenth-century Irish statesman and philosopher Edmund Burke is attributed with saying, "Evil triumphs when good men do nothing." My grandchildren's safety and opportunity to thrive depend on them being surrounded by men who accept the role for which they were created. When men obediently become the good stewards God created them to be, the Church flourishes because families are safe.

Be a Man

Together, we men of God can secure our society for the safety of our families, one man and one congregation at a time; however, each of us must choose to be fully committed to following Jesus and doing our part to secure the Kingdom of God. "Be the Man God Created" is the tagline for the Discipled Warriors Ministry. The ministry uses this tagline for multiple reasons, but let's conclude this lesson with Scripture that expresses the same mindset.

In Deuteronomy 31:7-8, Moses told Joshua—who would lead the nation of Israel into the Promised Land—to "Be strong and courageous, for you shall go with this people into the land that the Lord has sworn to their fathers to give them, and you shall put them in possession of it. It is the Lord who goes before you. He will be with you; he will not leave you or forsake you. Do not fear or be dismayed." In Joshua 1:9, God told Joshua to "Be strong and courageous. Do not be frightened, and do not be dismayed, for the Lord your God is with you wherever you go."

In 1 Kings 2:2-3, David told his son Solomon, "I am about to go the way of all the earth. So be strong, act like a man, and observe what the Lord your God requires: Walk in obedience to him, and keep his decrees and commands, his laws and regulations, as written in the Law of Moses. Do this so that you may prosper in all you do and wherever you go."

In 1 Corinthians 13:11, Paul stated, "When I was a child, I spoke like a child, I thought like a child, I reasoned like a child. When I became a man, I gave up childish ways." Later, in 1 Corinthians 16:13-14, he wrote, "Be watchful, stand firm in the faith, act like men, be strong. Let all that you do be done in love."

In Titus 1:7-9, Paul wrote, "God's steward must be above reproach. He must not be arrogant or quick-tempered or a drunkard or violent or greedy for gain, but hospitable, a lover of good, self-controlled, upright, holy, and disciplined. He must hold firm to the trustworthy word as taught, so that he may be able to give instruction in sound doctrine and also to rebuke those who contradict it."

As we close out the Discipled Warriors Handbook Lessons, I encourage you to *be the man God created* you to be. Choose to be a disciple of Jesus with a warrior's heart. Be righteous, obedient, strong, courageous, bold, loving, firm, honest, faithful, joyful, wise, and knowledgeable. Honor God. Love and protect your family. Spread the Gospel message and make disciples of all nations.

Lesson Application - Spiritual Gifts test

"Know yourself to lead yourself" is a phrase I picked up during a leadership course I once took. I like the phrase because it implies that a person must know not only their strengths and weaknesses but also their decision-making tendencies.

You will likely have a good idea of how your decisions will turn out. Ultimately, following God's will is how good decisions are made. However, there is no reason why we shouldn't use reliable and valid measurements to help us understand ourselves. First Peter 4:10 tells us that we have been given gifts to improve our stewardship of God's creation.

To know your gifts for free, take the Spiritual Gifts test at https://giftstest.com/test. The test will likely take fewer than ten minutes.

When you've completed the test, respond to the questions below.

What are your spiritual gifts?

What spiritual gifts do you use in your vocation?

How can you use your spiritual gifts to support the Church?

Conclusion

Final Applications

Congratulations on completing the Lesson Applications in the *Discipled Warriors Handbook*! The conclusion of the handbook requires you to conduct two more applications.

To complete the first one, review your responses to the previous 26 Lesson Applications to remind yourself of what you covered and learned. During your review, think about how you fit into the overall story of God's Kingdom to answer the question: Why are you here? Talk to God about your responses and listen to His Spirit to understand why you exist and how you fit in His Kingdom.

First Application - Using the space below, write a short explanation of the primary stewardship responsibilities God has given to you.

Second Application - Use the space below to write the most crucial task God wants you to achieve at this point in your life and why it is necessary for you to complete it.

About Kharis Publishing:

Kharis Publishing, an imprint of Kharis Media LLC, is a leading Christian and inspirational book publisher based in Aurora, Chicago metropolitan area, Illinois. Kharis' dual mission is to give voice to under-represented writers (including women and first-time authors) and equip orphans in developing countries with literacy tools. That is why, for each book sold, the publisher channels some of the proceeds into providing books and computers for orphanages in developing countries so that these kids may learn to read, dream, and grow. For a limited time, Kharis Publishing is accepting unsolicited queries for nonfiction (Christian, self-help, memoirs, business, health and wellness) from qualified leaders, professionals, pastors, and ministers. Learn more at: https://kharispublishing.com/

www.ingramcontent.com/pod-product-compliance
Lightning Source LLC
LaVergne TN
LVHW010612100826
845148LV00014B/2940
9781637466698